Journalism: A Very Short Introduction

VERY SHORT INTRODUCTIONS are for anyone wanting a stimulating and accessible way in to a new subject. They are written by experts, and have been translated into more than 40 different languages.

The Series began in 1995, and now covers a wide variety of topics in every discipline. The VSI library now contains over 350 volumes—a Very Short Introduction to everything from Psychology and Philosophy of Science to American History and Relativity—and continues to grow in every subject area.

Very Short Introductions available now:

ACCOUNTING Christopher Nobes
ADVERTISING Winston Fletcher
AFRICAN AMERICAN RELIGION Eddie S. Glaude Jr.
AFRICAN HISTORY John Parker and Richard Rathbone
AFRICAN RELIGIONS Jacob K. Olupona
AGNOSTICISM Robin Le Poidevin
ALEXANDER THE GREAT Hugh Bowden
AMERICAN HISTORY Paul S. Boyer
AMERICAN IMMIGRATION David A. Gerber
AMERICAN LEGAL HISTORY G. Edward White
AMERICAN POLITICAL PARTIES AND ELECTIONS L. Sandy Maisel
AMERICAN POLITICS Richard M. Valelly
THE AMERICAN PRESIDENCY Charles O. Jones
AMERICAN SLAVERY Heather Andrea Williams
ANAESTHESIA Aidan O'Donnell
ANARCHISM Colin Ward
ANCIENT EGYPT Ian Shaw
ANCIENT GREECE Paul Cartledge
THE ANCIENT NEAR EAST Amanda H. Podany
ANCIENT PHILOSOPHY Julia Annas
ANCIENT WARFARE Harry Sidebottom
ANGELS David Albert Jones
ANGLICANISM Mark Chapman
THE ANGLO-SAXON AGE John Blair
THE ANIMAL KINGDOM Peter Holland
ANIMAL RIGHTS David DeGrazia
THE ANTARCTIC Klaus Dodds
ANTISEMITISM Steven Beller
ANXIETY Daniel Freeman and Jason Freeman
THE APOCRYPHAL GOSPELS Paul Foster
ARCHAEOLOGY Paul Bahn
ARCHITECTURE Andrew Ballantyne
ARISTOCRACY William Doyle
ARISTOTLE Jonathan Barnes
ART HISTORY Dana Arnold
ART THEORY Cynthia Freeland
ASTROBIOLOGY David C. Catling
ATHEISM Julian Baggini
AUGUSTINE Henry Chadwick
AUSTRALIA Kenneth Morgan
AUTISM Uta Frith
THE AVANT GARDE David Cottington
THE AZTECS Davíd Carrasco
BACTERIA Sebastian G. B. Amyes
BARTHES Jonathan Culler
THE BEATS David Sterritt
BEAUTY Roger Scruton
BESTSELLERS John Sutherland
THE BIBLE John Riches
BIBLICAL ARCHAEOLOGY Eric H. Cline
BIOGRAPHY Hermione Lee
THE BLUES Elijah Wald
THE BOOK OF MORMON Terryl Givens

BORDERS Alexander C. Diener and Joshua Hagen
THE BRAIN Michael O'Shea
THE BRITISH CONSTITUTION Martin Loughlin
THE BRITISH EMPIRE Ashley Jackson
BRITISH POLITICS Anthony Wright
BUDDHA Michael Carrithers
BUDDHISM Damien Keown
BUDDHIST ETHICS Damien Keown
CANCER Nicholas James
CAPITALISM James Fulcher
CATHOLICISM Gerald O'Collins
CAUSATION Stephen Mumford and Rani Lill Anjum
THE CELL Terence Allen and Graham Cowling
THE CELTS Barry Cunliffe
CHAOS Leonard Smith
CHILDREN'S LITERATURE Kimberley Reynolds
CHINESE LITERATURE Sabina Knight
CHOICE THEORY Michael Allingham
CHRISTIAN ART Beth Williamson
CHRISTIAN ETHICS D. Stephen Long
CHRISTIANITY Linda Woodhead
CITIZENSHIP Richard Bellamy
CIVIL ENGINEERING David Muir Wood
CLASSICAL LITERATURE William Allan
CLASSICAL MYTHOLOGY Helen Morales
CLASSICS Mary Beard and John Henderson
CLAUSEWITZ Michael Howard
CLIMATE Mark Maslin
THE COLD WAR Robert McMahon
COLONIAL AMERICA Alan Taylor
COLONIAL LATIN AMERICAN LITERATURE Rolena Adorno
COMEDY Matthew Bevis
COMMUNISM Leslie Holmes
COMPLEXITY John H. Holland
THE COMPUTER Darrel Ince
CONFUCIANISM Daniel K. Gardner
THE CONQUISTADORS Matthew Restall and Felipe Fernández-Armesto
CONSCIENCE Paul Strohm
CONSCIOUSNESS Susan Blackmore
CONTEMPORARY ART Julian Stallabrass
CONTEMPORARY FICTION Robert Eaglestone
CONTINENTAL PHILOSOPHY Simon Critchley
CORAL REEFS Charles Sheppard
COSMOLOGY Peter Coles
CRITICAL THEORY Stephen Eric Bronner
THE CRUSADES Christopher Tyerman
CRYPTOGRAPHY Fred Piper and Sean Murphy
THE CULTURAL REVOLUTION Richard Curt Kraus
DADA AND SURREALISM David Hopkins
DARWIN Jonathan Howard
THE DEAD SEA SCROLLS Timothy Lim
DEMOCRACY Bernard Crick
DERRIDA Simon Glendinning
DESCARTES Tom Sorell
DESERTS Nick Middleton
DESIGN John Heskett
DEVELOPMENTAL BIOLOGY Lewis Wolpert
THE DEVIL Darren Oldridge
DIASPORA Kevin Kenny
DICTIONARIES Lynda Mugglestone
DINOSAURS David Norman
DIPLOMACY Joseph M. Siracusa
DOCUMENTARY FILM Patricia Aufderheide
DREAMING J. Allan Hobson
DRUGS Leslie Iversen
DRUIDS Barry Cunliffe
EARLY MUSIC Thomas Forrest Kelly
THE EARTH Martin Redfern
ECONOMICS Partha Dasgupta
EDUCATION Gary Thomas
EGYPTIAN MYTH Geraldine Pinch
EIGHTEENTH-CENTURY BRITAIN Paul Langford
THE ELEMENTS Philip Ball
EMOTION Dylan Evans
EMPIRE Stephen Howe
ENGELS Terrell Carver
ENGINEERING David Blockley
ENGLISH LITERATURE Jonathan Bate
ENTREPRENEURSHIP Paul Westhead and Mike Wright
ENVIRONMENTAL ECONOMICS Stephen Smith

EPIDEMIOLOGY Rodolfo Saracci
ETHICS Simon Blackburn
ETHNOMUSICOLOGY Timothy Rice
THE ETRUSCANS Christopher Smith
THE EUROPEAN UNION John Pinder and Simon Usherwood
EVOLUTION Brian and Deborah Charlesworth
EXISTENTIALISM Thomas Flynn
THE EYE Michael Land
FAMILY LAW Jonathan Herring
FASCISM Kevin Passmore
FASHION Rebecca Arnold
FEMINISM Margaret Walters
FILM Michael Wood
FILM MUSIC Kathryn Kalinak
THE FIRST WORLD WAR Michael Howard
FOLK MUSIC Mark Slobin
FOOD John Krebs
FORENSIC PSYCHOLOGY David Canter
FORENSIC SCIENCE Jim Fraser
FOSSILS Keith Thomson
FOUCAULT Gary Gutting
FRACTALS Kenneth Falconer
FREE SPEECH Nigel Warburton
FREE WILL Thomas Pink
FRENCH LITERATURE John D. Lyons
THE FRENCH REVOLUTION William Doyle
FREUD Anthony Storr
FUNDAMENTALISM Malise Ruthven
GALAXIES John Gribbin
GALILEO Stillman Drake
GAME THEORY Ken Binmore
GANDHI Bhikhu Parekh
GENES Jonathan Slack
GENIUS Andrew Robinson
GEOGRAPHY John Matthews and David Herbert
GEOPOLITICS Klaus Dodds
GERMAN LITERATURE Nicholas Boyle
GERMAN PHILOSOPHY Andrew Bowie
GLOBAL CATASTROPHES Bill McGuire
GLOBAL ECONOMIC HISTORY Robert C. Allen
GLOBAL WARMING Mark Maslin
GLOBALIZATION Manfred Steger
GOD John Bowker
THE GOTHIC Nick Groom
GOVERNANCE Mark Bevir
THE GREAT DEPRESSION AND THE NEW DEAL Eric Rauchway
HABERMAS James Gordon Finlayson
HAPPINESS Daniel M. Haybron
HEGEL Peter Singer
HEIDEGGER Michael Inwood
HERODOTUS Jennifer T. Roberts
HIEROGLYPHS Penelope Wilson
HINDUISM Kim Knott
HISTORY John H. Arnold
THE HISTORY OF ASTRONOMY Michael Hoskin
THE HISTORY OF LIFE Michael Benton
THE HISTORY OF MATHEMATICS Jacqueline Stedall
THE HISTORY OF MEDICINE William Bynum
THE HISTORY OF TIME Leofranc Holford-Strevens
HIV/AIDS Alan Whiteside
HOBBES Richard Tuck
HORMONES Martin Luck
HUMAN EVOLUTION Bernard Wood
HUMAN RIGHTS Andrew Clapham
HUMANISM Stephen Law
HUME A. J. Ayer
HUMOUR Noël Carroll
THE ICE AGE Jamie Woodward
IDEOLOGY Michael Freeden
INDIAN PHILOSOPHY Sue Hamilton
INFORMATION Luciano Floridi
INNOVATION Mark Dodgson and David Gann
INTELLIGENCE Ian J. Deary
INTERNATIONAL MIGRATION Khalid Koser
INTERNATIONAL RELATIONS Paul Wilkinson
INTERNATIONAL SECURITY Christopher S. Browning
ISLAM Malise Ruthven
ISLAMIC HISTORY Adam Silverstein
ITALIAN LITERATURE Peter Hainsworth and David Robey
JESUS Richard Bauckham
JOURNALISM Ian Hargreaves

JUDAISM Norman Solomon
JUNG Anthony Stevens
KABBALAH Joseph Dan
KAFKA Ritchie Robertson
KANT Roger Scruton
KEYNES Robert Skidelsky
KIERKEGAARD Patrick Gardiner
KNOWLEDGE Jennifer Nagel
THE KORAN Michael Cook
LANDSCAPE ARCHITECTURE Ian H. Thompson
LANDSCAPES AND GEOMORPHOLOGY Andrew Goudie and Heather Viles
LANGUAGES Stephen R. Anderson
LATE ANTIQUITY Gillian Clark
LAW Raymond Wacks
THE LAWS OF THERMODYNAMICS Peter Atkins
LEADERSHIP Keith Grint
LINCOLN Allen C. Guelzo
LINGUISTICS Peter Matthews
LITERARY THEORY Jonathan Culler
LOCKE John Dunn
LOGIC Graham Priest
MACHIAVELLI Quentin Skinner
MADNESS Andrew Scull
MAGIC Owen Davies
MAGNA CARTA Nicholas Vincent
MAGNETISM Stephen Blundell
MALTHUS Donald Winch
MANAGEMENT John Hendry
MAO Delia Davin
MARINE BIOLOGY Philip V. Mladenov
THE MARQUIS DE SADE John Phillips
MARTIN LUTHER Scott H. Hendrix
MARTYRDOM Jolyon Mitchell
MARX Peter Singer
MATHEMATICS Timothy Gowers
THE MEANING OF LIFE Terry Eagleton
MEDICAL ETHICS Tony Hope
MEDICAL LAW Charles Foster
MEDIEVAL BRITAIN John Gillingham and Ralph A. Griffiths
MEMORY Jonathan K. Foster
METAPHYSICS Stephen Mumford
MICHAEL FARADAY Frank A. J. L. James
MICROECONOMICS Avinash Dixit
MODERN ART David Cottington
MODERN CHINA Rana Mitter
MODERN FRANCE Vanessa R. Schwartz
MODERN IRELAND Senia Pašeta
MODERN JAPAN Christopher Goto-Jones
MODERN LATIN AMERICAN LITERATURE Roberto González Echevarría
MODERN WAR Richard English
MODERNISM Christopher Butler
MOLECULES Philip Ball
THE MONGOLS Morris Rossabi
MORMONISM Richard Lyman Bushman
MUHAMMAD Jonathan A. C. Brown
MULTICULTURALISM Ali Rattansi
MUSIC Nicholas Cook
MYTH Robert A. Segal
THE NAPOLEONIC WARS Mike Rapport
NATIONALISM Steven Grosby
NELSON MANDELA Elleke Boehmer
NEOLIBERALISM Manfred Steger and Ravi Roy
NETWORKS Guido Caldarelli and Michele Catanzaro
THE NEW TESTAMENT Luke Timothy Johnson
THE NEW TESTAMENT AS LITERATURE Kyle Keefer
NEWTON Robert Iliffe
NIETZSCHE Michael Tanner
NINETEENTH-CENTURY BRITAIN Christopher Harvie and H. C. G. Matthew
THE NORMAN CONQUEST George Garnett
NORTH AMERICAN INDIANS Theda Perdue and Michael D. Green
NORTHERN IRELAND Marc Mulholland
NOTHING Frank Close
NUCLEAR POWER Maxwell Irvine
NUCLEAR WEAPONS Joseph M. Siracusa
NUMBERS Peter M. Higgins
NUTRITION David A. Bender
OBJECTIVITY Stephen Gaukroger

THE OLD TESTAMENT
Michael D. Coogan
THE ORCHESTRA D. Kern Holoman
ORGANIZATIONS Mary Jo Hatch
PAGANISM Owen Davies
THE PALESTINIAN-ISRAELI
CONFLICT Martin Bunton
PARTICLE PHYSICS Frank Close
PAUL E. P. Sanders
PENTECOSTALISM William K. Kay
THE PERIODIC TABLE Eric R. Scerri
PHILOSOPHY Edward Craig
PHILOSOPHY OF LAW
Raymond Wacks
PHILOSOPHY OF SCIENCE
Samir Okasha
PHOTOGRAPHY Steve Edwards
PHYSICAL CHEMISTRY Peter Atkins
PLAGUE Paul Slack
PLANETS David A. Rothery
PLANTS Timothy Walker
PLATO Julia Annas
POLITICAL PHILOSOPHY
David Miller
POLITICS Kenneth Minogue
POSTCOLONIALISM Robert Young
POSTMODERNISM Christopher Butler
POSTSTRUCTURALISM
Catherine Belsey
PREHISTORY Chris Gosden
PRESOCRATIC PHILOSOPHY
Catherine Osborne
PRIVACY Raymond Wacks
PROBABILITY John Haigh
PROGRESSIVISM Walter Nugent
PROTESTANTISM Mark A. Noll
PSYCHIATRY Tom Burns
PSYCHOLOGY Gillian Butler and
Freda McManus
PURITANISM Francis J. Bremer
THE QUAKERS Pink Dandelion
QUANTUM THEORY
John Polkinghorne
RACISM Ali Rattansi
RADIOACTIVITY Claudio Tuniz
RASTAFARI Ennis B. Edmonds
THE REAGAN REVOLUTION Gil Troy
REALITY Jan Westerhoff
THE REFORMATION Peter Marshall
RELATIVITY Russell Stannard
RELIGION IN AMERICA Timothy Beal
THE RENAISSANCE Jerry Brotton
RENAISSANCE ART
Geraldine A. Johnson
REVOLUTIONS Jack A. Goldstone
RHETORIC Richard Toye
RISK Baruch Fischhoff and John Kadvany
RIVERS Nick Middleton
ROBOTICS Alan Winfield
ROMAN BRITAIN Peter Salway
THE ROMAN EMPIRE
Christopher Kelly
THE ROMAN REPUBLIC
David M. Gwynn
ROMANTICISM Michael Ferber
ROUSSEAU Robert Wokler
RUSSELL A. C. Grayling
RUSSIAN HISTORY Geoffrey Hosking
RUSSIAN LITERATURE Catriona Kelly
THE RUSSIAN REVOLUTION
S. A. Smith
SCHIZOPHRENIA Chris Frith and
Eve Johnstone
SCHOPENHAUER Christopher Janaway
SCIENCE AND RELIGION
Thomas Dixon
SCIENCE FICTION David Seed
THE SCIENTIFIC REVOLUTION
Lawrence M. Principe
SCOTLAND Rab Houston
SEXUALITY Véronique Mottier
SHAKESPEARE Germaine Greer
SIKHISM Eleanor Nesbitt
THE SILK ROAD James A. Millward
SLEEP Steven W. Lockley and
Russell G. Foster
SOCIAL AND CULTURAL
ANTHROPOLOGY
John Monaghan and Peter Just
SOCIALISM Michael Newman
SOCIOLINGUISTICS John Edwards
SOCIOLOGY Steve Bruce
SOCRATES C. C. W. Taylor
THE SOVIET UNION Stephen Lovell
THE SPANISH CIVIL WAR
Helen Graham
SPANISH LITERATURE Jo Labanyi
SPINOZA Roger Scruton
SPIRITUALITY Philip Sheldrake
STARS Andrew King

STATISTICS David J. Hand
STEM CELLS Jonathan Slack
STUART BRITAIN John Morrill
SUPERCONDUCTIVITY Stephen Blundell
SYMMETRY Ian Stewart
TEETH Peter S. Ungar
TERRORISM Charles Townshend
THEOLOGY David F. Ford
THOMAS AQUINAS Fergus Kerr
THOUGHT Tim Bayne
TIBETAN BUDDHISM Matthew T. Kapstein
TOCQUEVILLE Harvey C. Mansfield
TRAGEDY Adrian Poole
THE TROJAN WAR Eric H. Cline
TRUST Katherine Hawley
THE TUDORS John Guy
TWENTIETH-CENTURY BRITAIN Kenneth O. Morgan
THE UNITED NATIONS Jussi M. Hanhimäki
THE U.S. CONGRESS Donald A. Ritchie
THE U.S. SUPREME COURT Linda Greenhouse
UTOPIANISM Lyman Tower Sargent
THE VIKINGS Julian Richards
VIRUSES Dorothy H. Crawford
WITCHCRAFT Malcolm Gaskill
WITTGENSTEIN A. C. Grayling
WORK Stephen Fineman
WORLD MUSIC Philip Bohlman
THE WORLD TRADE ORGANIZATION Amrita Narlikar
WRITING AND SCRIPT Andrew Robinson

Available soon:

THEATRE Marvin Carlson
THE MIDDLE AGES Miri Rubin
STRUCTURAL ENGINEERING David Blockley
MINERALS David Vaughan
MATERIALS Christopher Hall
ANCIENT EGYPTIAN ART AND ARCHITECTURE Christina Riggs

For more information visit our website

www.oup.com/vsi/

Ian Hargreaves

JOURNALISM

A Very Short Introduction

SECOND EDITION

OXFORD
UNIVERSITY PRESS

Great Clarendon Street, Oxford, OX2 6DP,
United Kingdom

Oxford University Press is a department of the University of Oxford.
It furthers the University's objective of excellence in research, scholarship,
and education by publishing worldwide. Oxford is a registered trade mark of
Oxford University Press in the UK and in certain other countries

First published as Journalism: Truth or Dare, 2003
First published as a Very Short Introduction, 2005
Second edition, 2014

Published in the United States of America by Oxford University Press
198 Madison Avenue, New York, NY 10016, United States of America

British Library Cataloguing in Publication Data
Data available

Library of Congress Control Number: 2014937968

ISBN 978–0–19–968687–2

Printed and bound by
CPI Group (UK) Ltd, Croydon, CR0 4YY

To Ben, Kelda, Yoko, Zola, and Adele

Contents

Acknowledgements xv

List of illustrations xvii

Introduction: waiting for the endgame 1

1 Born free: a brief history of news media 8

2 Big Brother: journalism and the altered state 22

3 The first casualty: journalists at war 35

4 Star-struck: journalism as entertainment 50

5 Up to a point, Lord Copper's: who owns journalists? 62

6 Hacks vs flaks: journalism and public relations 78

7 Murder is my meat: the ethics of journalism 91

8 Digital: after the deluge 108

Further reading 141

Index 145

Acknowledgements

Countless people have contributed to the thinking in these pages, especially my fellow-journalists at the *Keighley News*, the Bradford *Telegraph and Argus*, the *Financial Times*, the BBC, the *Independent*, and the *New Statesman*, my main homes in a 30-year career in the news business.

The motivation for the book, however, arose from my links with Cardiff University, where I initially worked alongside Professor John Hartley, then Head of the School of Journalism, Media and Cultural Studies. Professional journalists, especially British ones, are given to disdain the work of media scholars like Hartley; but my time in Cardiff convinced me that journalists would do a better job for the citizens and causes they serve if they engaged more constructively with critical interrogation. This slim volume in its first edition aimed to contribute to that process. The second edition, a decade later, continues in that vein, amid the severe disruptions to the news business occasioned by the Internet.

Cardiff
May 2014

List of illustrations

1 The ten deadliest countries for journalists **9**
Data from Committee to Protect Journalists (https://www.cpj.org/)

2 World press freedom map **11**
By permission of Freedom House

3 Tiananmen Square **28**
Arthur Tsang/Reuters/Corbis

4 The Vietnam War **37**
Eddie Adams/AP/Press Association Images

5 *Daily Telegraph* front page: 9/11 **42**
Telegraph Media Group Limited 2011/Photo Spencer Platt/Getty Images

6 Al Jazeera America **48**
Saul Loeb/AFP/Getty Images

7 Princess Diana and paparazzi **56**
Rex Features

8 Jeff Bezos, founder of Amazon, purchases the *Washington Post* **63**
David Brabyn/Corbis

9 World's top ten media companies **66**
Zenith Optimedia 2013, using 2011 data

10 Rupert Murdoch in 1969, after acquiring the *News of the World* **70**
Stan Meagher/Getty Images

11 *All the President's Men* **92**
Ronald Grant Archive

12 Front page of last *News of the World*, 2011 **105**
Tony Kyriacou/Rex Features

13 The decade of decline: circulations between *c.*2000 and *c.*2012 for UK and US national newspapers **112**

a) American Society of News Editors annual census

b) ABC data, author's interpretation based upon national newspaper sales of editons Monday to Saturday

14 Matt Drudge **117**
Art Garrison

15 Digital news around the world **131**
By permission of Reuters Institute for the Study of Journalism/University of Oxford

16 Julian Assange, founder of WikiLeaks **133**
David Levenson/Getty Images

Introduction: waiting for the endgame

Journalism entered the 21st century caught in a paradox. The world had more journalism, across a wider range of media, than at any time since the birth of the Western free press in the 18th century. Experts debated whether this flowering was the cause or the result of the political changes signalled by the fall of the Berlin Wall in 1990. The resulting globalization carried some version of market economics and liberalizing politics to almost every corner of the planet. According to one theory of its time, this marked the resolution of the bipolar ideological struggle between communism and capitalism: in the words of the political scientist Francis Fukuyama: the 'end of history'.

For journalists, things did not seem so clear cut. Western journalists found themselves simultaneously under a cloud of suspicion: from politicians, philosophers, the general public, anti-globalization radicals, religious groups, and even from some journalists. Critics argued that the West's, and especially America's, commercially-funded news industry had lost its moral and civic bearings, focusing too much on high investment returns for shareholders, achieved through serving up celebrity, entertainment, and escapism ('infotainment'), rather than reporting and analysing the more taxing political, economic, and social issues of the day.

This debate obscured the fact that a much mightier storm was brewing, as the digital technologies associated with the Internet started to throw up entirely new global platforms capable of delivering online news, in all media, along with new platforms to reach advertisers. At the turn of the millennium, as the stock market overheated and the 'dot-com bubble' burst, some still questioned the scale of this wave of change, with the result that many prestigious news organizations sleepwalked into what would become the Western news industry's most difficult decade for more than a century.

In these years, the digital 'communications revolution' all but destroyed the dominant advertising-based industrial model for newspaper journalism, undermining profits, eliminating jobs, and closing titles. No longer was it possible for regional and local newspapers to make money by selling pages of 'classified' advertising for jobs, houses, cars, and other items, interleaved with news, when instantly searchable web-based lists provided a better and more efficient service. The advertising revenues of US newspapers fell every year between 2005 and 2013, and between 2000 and 2012 the number of people employed in American newsrooms fell by 30 per cent. Things were made worse by the onset of economic recession in 2008, following the New York banking crisis.

Nor was it only the newspaper business model which suffered trauma. Google's dominant search system also made it possible to reach audiences in new ways, aggregating news and related factual material instantly from many sources, providing a rich experience for audiences, whilst simultaneously enabling Google to sell ads against this traffic. The result was that those reliant on established business models of creating and distributing news took most of the pain of the emerging technology, whilst new, 'born-digital' players harvested the gain. Apple, leader in the booming tablet and smartphone market, established itself as a middleman for news organizations selling content via its 'app store'. In August 2013, Jeff Bezos, founder of Amazon, a digital platform which started in books but went on to dominate online retailing, completed the dance of overturned tables by buying the *Washington Post* for $250 million. Soon after, Pierre Omidyar, the founder of eBay, set up a platform for investigative journalism as new, online news providers like Buzzfeed and Vice carved distinctive niches.

As disaster piled upon disaster for the 'legacy' news industry, the gloomiest American critics proclaimed the end not only of well-resourced, independent, professional journalism but of America's democratic polity, which it was said could not prosper without a robust 'fourth estate' to hold politicians and others to account.

Against this pessimism, two qualifying points must be made. The first is that the United States is both important and exceptional in the story of journalism. In 2013, Indian newspapers continued to experience strong growth in sales, as they opened up new markets in vernacular (non-English) languages to meet the demands of an increasingly literate population in a marketplace where newspaper penetration had not yet reached 15 per cent and where broadband infrastructure is weak. Likewise, the dynamics of the huge and politically complex Chinese market, where advertising-led business models were successfully established only in the first decade of the new millennium, bear little resemblance to the media markets of North America. Even Europe's news system, which shares strong philosophical roots with America, has been protected by its long tradition of taxpayer-funded public service broadcasting and a willingness (for example in some Scandinavian countries) to provide subsidies for newspapers. In the UK, the BBC's 'licence fee' income, worth in excess of £3.5 billion in 2013, has enabled the broadcaster to establish itself as a leading global provider of online news services, whilst maintaining its hold on public trust as the UK's most trusted provider of news.

The second qualification is that even in the turbulent news media markets of North America there is more than one way of reading what is going on. Optimists see the networked information ecology still emerging around the Internet as a highly promising, collaborative response to the news industry's previously diagnosed malaise. This 'networked public sphere' or 'fifth estate' uses new technologies to make the collection and distribution of news quicker, cheaper, multimedia, and global. It also raises money in new ways, offering journalism that is less dependent on big advertisers and more open to new interests and voices, more 'plural'. Hyperlocal online journalists can serve geographical communities previously too small to support commercial media, whilst a new global journalism can stretch its horizons in new partnerships with experts and activists, yielding an enhanced flow of 'long-form' journalism. In this redefined online news ecology, professional journalists are still important as reporters, commentators, editors, and curators, but they are no longer unchallenged authorities; they must collaborate.

The first edition of this book was written at the opening of this turbulent first decade of the new century, when the questions facing journalism in the digital communications revolution were only just starting to come into focus. Google was not yet a public company and Facebook was not born. News bloggers had started to make an impact and media companies were eyeing each other warily as digital technology promised 'convergence' on common platforms. In the United States, journalists frustrated by their bosses' focus on profits and mergers launched a 'public journalism' movement, committed to journalism of higher civic purpose. In the Arab world, Al Jazeera emerged as a powerful force in the Arab Street. President Putin, the former KGB man, had just taken office in Russia, with undisclosed ideas of his own about news media matters, following the chaotic exit of his predecessor Boris Yeltsin.

In constructing this second edition, my aim, as in the first, is to inform the general reader about what journalism has been, what it is, and what it might become. I have retained the shape and much content from the first edition in order to retest its arguments in these altered times.

I begin with history (Chapter 1) followed by a discussion of the role of the state in journalism (Chapter 2). My outline of journalism's history and its entanglement with the adventure of democratization owe much to John Keane's writings on democracy, which influenced both editions of this book. Particularly welcome is Keane's debunking of the idea that democracy is an exclusively Western franchise. His counter-proposition is that in our own age of communicative abundance, we should think beyond parliamentary or representative democracy to a 'monitory democracy', composed of a shifting ecology of agencies, watchdogs, activists, informants, journalists, and experts, helping to strengthen the ways in which we hold power to account. Although Keane is rightly suspicious of utopian claims for the tools of digital communication, he sides cautiously with the techno-optimists in saying that 'communicative abundance on balance has positive consequences. In spite of all its hype and spin, the new media galaxy nudges and broadens people's horizons. It tutors their sense of pluralism and prods them into taking greater responsibility for how, when and why they communicate.'

From there I move to considering journalism and war (Chapter 3), an aspect of the news industry transformed by technology and events, especially those wars in Afghanistan and Iraq which followed the terrorist attacks on New York and Washington on 11 September 2001. Media scholars argue that the conduct of war itself has been changed by the resulting 'mediatization' of these and other conflicts.

Chapter 4 considers journalism's 'tabloid' instinct: its pursuit of a mass audience via entertainment and a much-criticized obsession with celebrity. Chapter 5 explores issues of news media ownership, noting the decline of the press baron, and Chapter 6 the relationship between journalism and what some journalists call the 'dark side'—public relations. Each of these themes points towards ethical issues, which are discussed in Chapter 7, including reflections on the UK phone-hacking scandal, which resulted in the appointment of a judicial inquiry into the culture, practices, and ethics of the press: the Leveson inquiry in 2011.

The final chapter draws together developments in digital journalism and makes judgements about where these might be heading. In the first edition, there was a substantial walk-on part for Matt Drudge, the American West Coast blogger and breaker of a scandal which befell President Clinton following his relationship with Monica Lewinsky, a White House intern. Drudge retains his place in these pages, bookended with a potentially much more significant figure; Julian Assange, the founder of WikiLeaks, and his reverberation: the secret service leaker, Edward Snowden. Although a detailed account of all important international developments is beyond the scope of such a short book, I try to reflect developments in China, Russia, India, South America, and the Arab world, as well as covering Europe and North America as fully as possible.

My perspective is that of the journalist turned academic—a breed which has come to be known, not entirely flatteringly, as the 'hackademic'. I started, after university, as a local newspaper reporter in northern England and then spent a decade reporting for the *Financial Times*, then one of the world's few global newspapers. I ran the BBC's vast news and current affairs operation during a period of its reinvigoration in the late 1980s before becoming in succession deputy editor of the *Financial Times*, editor of the *Independent*, and editor of the *New Statesman*, a great political weekly founded by Fabian Socialists nearly a century before I got there. My academic home is Cardiff University, which accommodates Britain's oldest journalism school. In the last decade, I have also worked as director of corporate affairs for a major UK company, as director of strategic communications for the UK Foreign and Commonwealth Office, and as a founding non-executive director of Ofcom, the UK's converged communications regulator. In 2010, I took up a new role at Cardiff University, where I am Professor of Digital Economy, focused on understanding the effects of digital technologies on the creative economy, which includes journalism.

These diverse experiences are what primarily inform this book, along with what is now an extensive academic literature on journalism. In recent years, it has sometimes seemed as if there are more journalists in universities than in newspapers, but this, I assure myself, is an optical illusion. What I have learned most clearly from my own experience is that we need competing cultures of ownership and practice if our news media are to be truly diverse and widely trusted. We need journalism that does not seek power on its own account, but which has the explicit goal of empowering others. We also need journalism that has the resources to do its work effectively and which undertakes its responsibilities honestly and accountably.

Journalism's job is to provide the information and argument that enable societies to establish facts, to work through disagreements, to test moral boundaries, and to know their priorities. It holds all power to account, including publishers and Internet magnates. Unlike poetry, which as W. H. Auden said, 'makes nothing happen' and 'survives in the valley of its making where executives would never want to tamper', journalism in all its forms demands a response. Executives and politicians will always want to tamper with the work of journalists, whether they are newspaper reporters, lone bloggers, industrial-scale leakers, or providers of global television news. These are the pressures that motivate journalism's mission and interrogate its moral standing.

Chapter 1
Born free: a brief history of news media

Before considering a chronology of journalism, let us pause to acknowledge the remorseless fatality rate among journalists whose work brings them into conflict with sources of power. In the last decade almost 600 journalists have been killed, chiefly in wars, in acts of political assassination or by gangsters. This figure excludes a large number of other media workers, such as researchers and translators, who also lost their lives working alongside journalists. The number of deaths goes up in times and places of particularly intense violence, such as in Syria and Egypt during 2012–13 or Iraq and Afghanistan in the previous decade.

The roll call of most dangerous places for journalists has been topped in recent years by Iraq, the Philippines, Algeria, Russia, Pakistan, and Somalia. But journalists also come under attack in less obviously troubled places. In early 2013, Rodrigo Neto, a 38-year-old radio host and reporter on a regional Brazilian daily who specialized in investigating police corruption, was gunned down from a motorcycle when leaving a barbecue: one of three linked Brazilian journalists shot dead in the opening weeks of that year. Daniel Pearl, a *Wall Street Journal* reporter, was working in Pakistan when he was kidnapped and murdered. The resulting propaganda video, showing a man brandishing a severed head, was then handed to American officials and posted on the Internet,

The ten deadliest countries for journalists

Country	Confirmed killings 1992–2012
Iraq	151
Philippines	73
Algeria	60
Russia	55
Pakistan	52
Somalia	50
Columbia	44
Syria	39
India	29
Mexico	28

1. Journalism continues to be a dangerous business as the powerful strike back

where at the time of writing it still lingers. Pearl's story would later be retold in a 2007 Hollywood film, *A Mighty Heart*.

According to the Committee to Protect Journalists, 42 per cent of the journalists killed since it started collating this data in 1992 were covering politics; and 35 per cent were reporting wars (see Figure 1). Freedom House, an American agency which has been monitoring press freedom around the world since 1980, perhaps too hastily labelled the 20th century 'the democratic century'. By 2012, Freedom House was logging a decline in the proportion of countries enjoying a free press: from 40 to 32 per cent across the decade. It commented:

> The trend of overall decline occurred, paradoxically, in a context of increasingly diverse news sources and ever-expanding means of political communication. The growth of these new media has triggered a repressive backlash by authoritarian regimes that have carefully controlled television and other mass media and are now alert to the dangers of unfettered political commentary online.

Influential powers—such as China, Russia, Iran and Venezuela—have long resorted to a variety of techniques to maintain a tight grip on the media, detaining some press critics, closing down or otherwise censoring media outlets and blogs and bringing libel or defamation suits against journalists.

New entrants to the 'not free' category in Freedom House's 2012 assessment included Ecuador, Egypt, Guinea-Bissau, Paraguay, and Thailand. Economic crisis in Europe also led to press freedom downgrades for Greece and Spain. This is the contemporary prologue to our brief history (see Figure 2).

From Gutenberg to Zuckerberg

Scholars do not agree about when 'journalism' started. Intuitively, it is hard to believe that any human society operated without transmission mechanisms for the latest information, the most urgent warnings, the most compelling gossip, and the most entertaining factual stories.

Sociologist Michael Schudson says that 'the primary institutional and cultural features of contemporary news have a relatively brief history—400 years at the outside. People have been paid to write true stories about current events and to publish them on a regular basis only for about 250 years, and, in many places, for more like 150 years.' We also know, however, that China had official information sheets (*tipao*) centuries before the years of democratizing revolution in Europe and America, spawning unofficial rivals of sufficient enterprise that the Sung dynasty (960–1279) felt it necessary to suppress them.

What can be agreed is that the invention of a printing technology, known as moveable type, by Johannes Gutenberg in Germany in the middle of the 15th century laid the groundwork for mass printing, without which journalism in the sense that Schudson defines it could not have happened. Although Gutenberg's initial customers

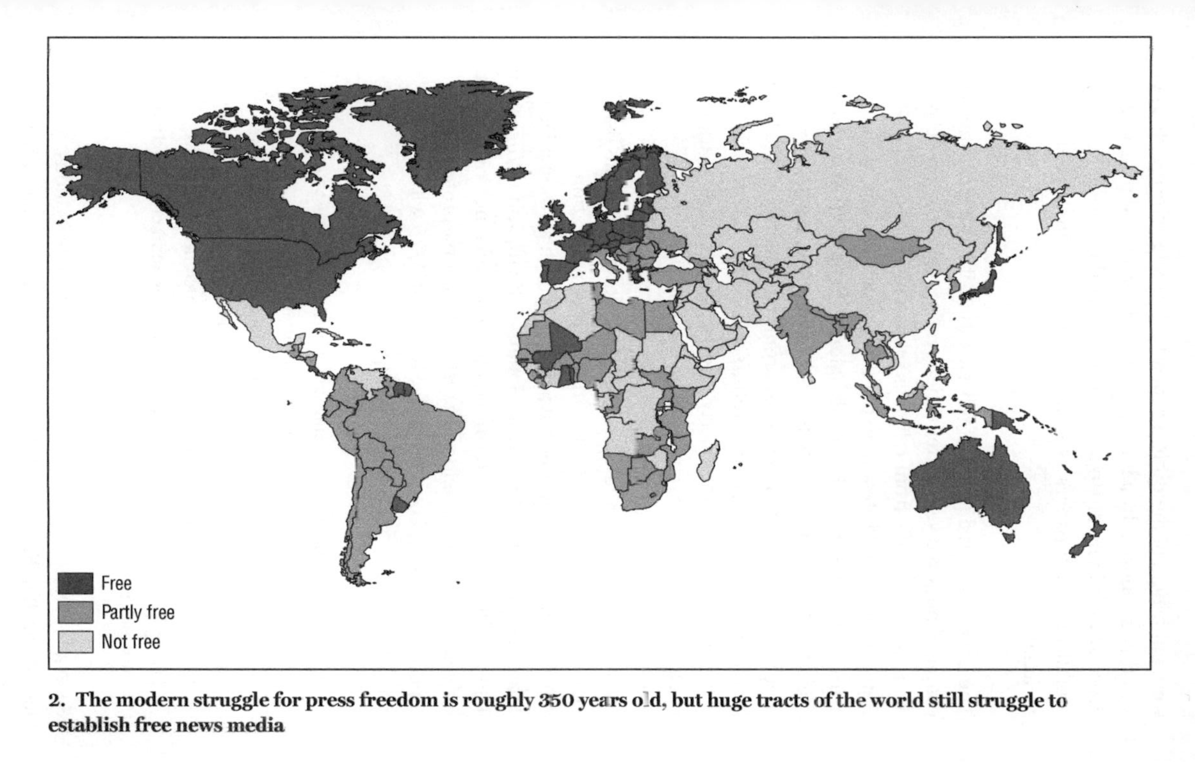

2. The modern struggle for press freedom is roughly 350 years old, but huge tracts of the world still struggle to establish free news media

were publishers of the Bible, his new tools made printing cheaper and this, supported by a long-run rise in literacy and prosperity, drove growth in newspaper markets all over the world, establishing newspapers as a throwaway item in industrial societies.

The Europe-centred phase of this narrative of modernity starts a couple of hundred years after Gutenberg's breakthrough, deriving its political dynamic from religious schism in Europe, where the Reformation saw Protestants split from what they saw as the censorious authority of Rome. Religion also marked divisions in the English Civil War (1642–8), when dissenting republicans toppled a monarch, spurred on by argument made possible by an increasingly free press. John Milton's *Areopagitica* famously proclaimed: 'Give me the liberty to know, to utter and to argue freely according to conscience, above all liberties.'

From there it was a small step to the first flowering of English journalism. Boosted by the abolition of pre-publication censorship, diversely motivated journalists such as Daniel Defoe, Joseph Addison, Richard Steele, Jonathan Swift, John Wilkes, and Thomas Paine became men of national and, in Paine's case, global influence. We owe to Defoe a snapshot of the first professional reporters, working London's coffee houses in 1728 with a ruthlessly commercial craftsmanship:

> Persons are employed... to haunt coffee houses and thrust themselves into companies where they are not known; or plant themselves at convenient distances to overhear what is said... The same persons hang and loiter about the publick offices like housebreakers, waiting for an interview with some little clerk or a conference with a door keeper in order to come at a little news, or an account of transactions; for which the fee is a shilling, or a pint of wine.

Soon after Defoe's time, the embryonic London news industry located itself in Fleet Street, a dingy thoroughfare named after the open sewer which connected the capital's business district to the east with the seat of political power in the west: symbolic of journalism's pivotal position in the country's emerging power structures.

Thomas Paine's journalistic work fomented revolution on both sides of the Atlantic. He sailed for Philadelphia in 1774 and two years later published *Common Sense*, a pamphlet setting out the case for American independence from British rule. The next year Paine returned to England and wrote *Rights of Man*, arguing that human beings have a natural right to govern themselves. Arraigned for treason, he fled to Paris and was elected a deputy in the National Convention, before being swept aside by revolutionary factionalism, which led to imprisonment and, almost, to his death. Paine returned to the United States, where he lived out his days on the uneasy border between political power and journalism in an era when factional loyalty was crucial to the identity of newspapers. Paine died in New York in 1809, refusing with his last breath to express belief in the divinity of Jesus Christ.

Milton's brooding spirit, Defoe's worldly professionalism, and Paine's rabble-rousing radicalism are reflected in the First Amendment to the American Constitution, which states that 'Congress shall make no law…abridging the freedom of speech or of the press', a momentously important linkage between the individual right of free expression and the liberties owing to the dominant news medium of the day. Thomas Jefferson reinforced the point when he wrote in 1787 to Colonel Edward Carrington the most comforting words in the history of journalism, that 'The basis of our government being the opinion of the people, the very first object should be to keep that right; and were it left to me to decide whether we should have a government without newspapers, or newspapers without a government, I should not hesitate a moment to prefer the latter.'

Amid the bloodier footprints of the French Revolution, Paine's influence left subtly different tracks. This was a political maelstrom which thrust many journalists into mainstream politics, with all the attendant risks. Editor and politician Jean Paul Marat was murdered in his bath, leaving for posterity a copy of his newspaper stained with his own blood. According to the historian Jack Richard Censer, the radical newspapermen of the revolutionary period 'generally saw themselves as politicians with a primary responsibility to influence the course of events and with little allegiance toward any abstract journalistic ethic'. This legacy touches French journalism today. France's journalism, with its roots in the political tract and the essay more than the witnessed news report, tends to be more intellectually adventurous and, some would say, serious than its Anglo-Saxon counterpart, but it is also less empirically forensic. French journalism is also more sensitive to the privacy of individuals: soft, say its Anglo-Saxon critics (pointing to the presidencies of Nicolas Sarkozy and François Hollande); grown-up, say its advocates.

On liberty

As British influence spread globally through empire, liberal values would leave important traces. James Mill, the Scots utilitarian, argued in an influential essay in 1811 that the dangers of a timorous press, too friendly to established political power, greatly exceeded the political dangers of its opposite. Almost half a century later, Mill's son, the philosopher John Stuart Mill, delivered the most eloquent case for free speech in the English language. In his 1859 essay *On Liberty* he writes:

> The peculiar evil of silencing an expression of opinion is that it is robbing the human race; posterity as well as the existing generation; those who dissent from the opinion, still more than those who hold it. If the opinion is right, they are deprived of the opportunity of exchanging error for truth: if wrong, they lose, what is almost as great a benefit, the clearer perception and livelier impression of truth, produced by its collision with error.

Liberals were thus friends of press freedom, philosophically, politically, and commercially. They opposed special taxes or stamp duties on newspapers as vigorously as they supported greater freedom to trade. In some countries, including the young republic of the United States of America, newspapers even attracted financial privileges, such as exemption from postal charges.

The upshot was a proliferation of titles in what is sometimes seen as the golden era of the press: politically radical but not yet, in the early stages of the Industrial Revolution, intensely focused upon mass markets and commercial returns. In Britain, Henry Hetherington's *Poor Man's Guardian*, launched in 1831, in defiance of stamp duty, declared: 'It is the cause of the rabble we advocate, the poor, the suffering, the industrious, the productive classes... We will teach this rabble their power—we will teach them that they are your master, instead of being your slaves.' Yet only two years after this launch, Hetheringon was also promising readers of his *Twopenny Dispatch* a diet of 'murders, rapes, suicides, burnings, maimings, theatricals, races, pugilism and... every sort of devilment that will make it sell'. Thus, in England, did the lion of radical political journalism settle down early alongside the crowd-pleasing lamb of tabloid sensationalism.

Before long, bigger newspapers, free from taxation and fat with advertising, were trumpeting the glories of a 'new journalism'. In 1852, *The Times* defined as its purpose: 'to obtain the earliest and most correct intelligence of the events of the time and instantly, by disclosing them, to make them the common property of the nation'. By now, papers like *The Times* could draw upon the resources of news agencies, such as the one launched by Julius Reuter in 1851.

Government by journalism

All of this prefigured the era of Big Media power of the 20th century. The embodiment of what British Victorian intellectuals called 'New Journalism' was W. T. Stead, editor of the *Pall Mall*

Gazette, who specialized in controversial exposures of sex rackets, as a result of which he found himself in Holloway Prison. From there in 1886 Stead wrote a remarkable essay, informing the world that journalism had now become 'superior to that of any other institution or profession known among men'. For Stead, the journalist was the key to comprehending public opinion, 'to be both eye and ear for the community':

> The journalist would speak with an authority far superior to that possessed by any other person; for he would have been the latest to interrogate the democracy. Parliament has attained its utmost development. There is need of a new representative method, not to supersede but to supplement that which exists—a system which will be more elastic, more simple, more direct and more closely in contact with the mind of the people... When the time does arrive, and the man and the money are both forthcoming, government by journalism will no longer be a somewhat hyperbolic phrase, but a solid fact.

This early techno-utopianism foreshadowed in the 20th century not only the dramatic growth of mass markets for newspapers, but also the rise of professional public relations, ambitious programmes of government propaganda, and the emergence of a range of electronic media. Stead's hubris was in tune with an era when newspapers were launched not with soberly descriptive titles such as *The Times*, *The Gazette*, and *The Record*, but ablaze with popular aspiration: the *Mirror*, the *Sun*, the *Comet*, and the *Star*. Most of Britain's great popular newspapers of today were born in the final years of Queen Victoria's reign or just afterwards: the *Daily Mail* (1896), the *Daily Express* (1900), and the *Daily Mirror* (1903).

Parallel forces were at work in the United States, where proprietors like William Randolph Hearst and Joseph Pulitzer presided over 'yellow' press titles, the *New York Journal* and *The New York Post*, adopting the latest printing technologies and building circulations which vastly exceeded those of the previous era. The newspaper industries of Britain and the United States thus entered the 20th century at the summit of their powers. They commanded mass audiences and could present themselves to politicians as 'independent' platforms through which politicians could, indeed must, engage with voters.

Out of this, in the first decades of the new century, would emerge a distinctive newspaper-owning class: publishers, often with political as well as commercial ambitions; but also a distinctive culture of journalistic professionalism, reflected in the birth in 1922 of the American Society of Newspaper Editors, and shortly afterwards the first journalism schools and early scholarly critiques of journalism and other popular media. Codified professional standards established the principle of 'objectivity' in reporting, in Michael Schudson's words, 'a natural and progressive ideology for an aspiring occupational group at a moment when science was God, efficiency was cherished and increasingly prominent elites judged partisanship a vestige of the tribal nineteenth century'. Walter Lippmann, a distinguished newspaper columnist and advisor to more than one president of the United States, said journalism was an essential interlocutor between government and a general public either too little educated or too little inclined to comprehend the intricacies of an increasingly complex world. This elitist perspective was challenged by John Dewey's more confident communitarian account of democracy's resilience. The Lippman–Dewey dialectic proved to be a continuingly illuminating point of reflection, as the newspaper age gave way to the dominance of electronic mass media.

Media monopoly, communism, and fascism

Within a couple of decades of the new century, the market-based model for the development of news media came under challenge, first from radio, then from television. These were media which would quickly acquire a reach never achievable by newspapers and they were born not in tiny printers' shops, subject to the laws of an emerging market economy and face-to-face transactions; rather, they were inventions easily and speedily commandeered by governments, which mostly took the view that the technology platforms on which they relied were scarce resources of such major importance that they must be owned or at the very least licensed by the state. It is too easily forgotten that the media technologies of the first half of the 20th century had their roots not in markets but in monopoly and licensed oligopoly, shaped and defined in a period of revolutionary politics.

The implications for journalism would be far reaching as governments sought through direct control or through the medium of 'independent' regulatory bodies to define the public interest to be served by these new media. Here, America and Europe would take divergent paths.

In Europe, the preferred model was invariably some kind of state- or public-ownership model for radio and later for television. For the United Kingdom, this meant the creation, in 1922, of the British Broadcasting Company, the world's first national broadcasting organization. Under the leadership of its first director general, John Reith, the BBC established itself around a mission to 'inform, educate and entertain', paid for by a tax on first radio- and then television-set ownership (the 'licence fee'). There was, from the start, a strong implied commitment to journalism, though in its earliest years, the BBC was not allowed to carry news before 7 pm, in order to avoid competition with newspapers. These rules were relaxed only when the 1926 General Strike closed down newspapers, enabling the BBC to start building what has become a uniquely trusted relationship with its news audiences. Then, as now, the BBC's journalism was required to show 'due impartiality' with regard to coverage of politics, public policy, and industrial issues, though Reith himself famously qualified this in a 1926 diary entry to the effect that 'they know that they can trust us not to be really impartial'. A version of these requirements was copied over to commercial television in the 1950s, ensuring that commercial terrestrial, cable, and satellite television in the UK was shaped by a sustained regulatory view of the character of broadcast journalism.

In the United States, it was a different story. Here, commercially-funded radio and television stations required a licence from the Federal Communications Commission (FCC, established in 1934) to use publicly owned radio spectrum. But as advertising revenues boomed, the advertisers and commercial sponsors wanted to reach the largest possible audience. Nor did they want taxpayer-funded competition, ensuring that America's publicly funded broadcasting alternative, PBS, would remain a marginal player.

In the first era of commercial broadcasting, the US networks established themselves as powerhouse businesses and opened up what would become a programme of heavy investment in news and current affairs, creating stars like CBS reporter Ed Murrow and newscaster Walter Cronkite. Murrow's reports from London during the Second World War and his television show's exposure of Senator Joseph McCarthy hold their place in journalism's hall of fame, but by 1961 President Kennedy's appointee to the chairmanship of the FCC, Newton Minow, felt it necessary to warn television bosses of their 'inescapable duty' to provide intelligent and aspirational programmes rather than the 'vast wasteland' of the schedules of the day. This produced a flurry of response, including the launch in 1968 of CBS's flagship current affairs show, 60 *Minutes*, and what some depict as a 'golden age' of American TV journalism. But it was short-lived: only 20 years after Minow's 'wasteland' speech, Mark Fowler, appointed to the FCC chairmanship by Republican president Ronald Reagan, would proclaim that 'the perception of broadcasters as community trustees should be replaced by a view of broadcasters as marketplace participants. Communications policy should be directed toward maximizing the services the public desires... [T]he public's interest, then, defines the public interest.'

As the age of broadcasting gave way to the age of the Internet, this market-reliant, deregulatory approach would become even more strongly held, anchored, according to its supporters, in the First Amendment to the Constitution, requiring the federal authorities to steer clear of any action dangerous to freedom of expression. These views found a strong echo in the UK during the prime ministership of Margaret Thatcher (1979–90), which deliberately challenged the dominance of the BBC by supporting the emergence of new non-profit competitors (Channel 4) and new private sector players—Rupert Murdoch's Sky Television, which rapidly established a dominant position in the growing pay television market. Murdoch, meanwhile, had established sufficient leverage in the USA to launch in 1986 Fox Broadcasting, a fourth television network.

Views differ sharply on the result of these differing approaches to the regulation of broadcasting and its impact upon news. In the United States, the Reagan/Bush presidencies are blamed for turning a blind eye to a sharp drop in resources devoted to broadcast news, especially to international reporting, with the result (according to some research) that many Americans lacked the information to grasp the basic political facts behind the terrorist attacks on New York and Washington in September 2001 (9/11). Deregulation also sanctioned more strident and factional political voices in broadcasting. Others maintain that the dominant role played subsequently by American technology companies in the emergence of the Internet, a global ecosystem promoting innovation in news, supports the view that the best results arise when government is least involved.

History has shaped news media cultures very differently from place to place. Take the example of modern Japan, where the press enjoys the protection of a national constitution which enshrines the principle of press freedom, established under strong American influence after the Second World War. But the workings of Japanese news media are barely recognizable to journalists from the United States or Britain. Japanese society works through negotiation, collaboration, and consensus rather than through strong ideological difference and competition. Japanese journalists are bound together in a network of a thousand 'press clubs', all linked to major institutional or industrial sources of power and therefore of news. These clubs are designed to ensure that both sides play by a set of unofficial rules. It is, in essence, a form of self-regulation, designed to avoid embarrassment and misunderstanding, but which in the opinion of its (mostly Western) critics neuters and homogenizes Japan's journalism through management of news.

If Japan is an example of relative political stability in terms of the climate of news media regulation in the last half century, Russia provides a case of the opposite. In the next chapter, we look at post-Cold War Russia to explore the diversity of ways in which today's nation states are responding to the emergence of the global media structures of the digital age.

Chapter 2
Big Brother: journalism and the altered state

In the early years of the 21st century, I spent some time in Russia, talking to journalists. They had come together to imbibe good practice from the democratic societies towards which post-Cold War liberalization had pointed them.

In most respects, the evangelism was welcomed. No one could or did defend the deceitful propaganda of the 'information regimes' of the Soviet era, when the titles of leading newspapers such as *Pravda* ('Truth') became grim self-parodies. Yet, as I joined the discussion, I couldn't avoid a sense of irony at the moralizing rhetoric of these mainly American news media people at a time when American journalism was widely accused of struggling with its own sense of civic purpose. By the year 2000, it was by no means obvious that capitalism's preferred model of unfettered shareholder-owned big business offered a universal model for sustaining free and inquiring news media.

Rupert Murdoch, the Australian-American publisher with an empire across four continents, did not agree. He likened the impact of nascent communications technologies of cable and satellite TV and the emerging Internet to the abolition of pre-publication censorship by the English Parliament in 1694, saying: 'They have proved an unambiguous threat to totalitarian regimes everywhere.' Not long afterwards, in 2000, President Bill

Clinton was asked about the risk that China might set about controlling the Internet in the way its Communist Party controlled newspapers and broadcasting. He replied that this would be unimaginable, 'like nailing Jell-O to the wall'.

After the Cold War

Holed up as I was at a Soviet-era conference centre on the edge of snowbound Moscow, here was my chance to talk to senior figures from the still young Russian Parliament, the Duma, the state television authorities, the Moscow press, and a group of young but by no means inexperienced journalists from across Russia. At issue was the kind of journalism developing in Russia, as it struggled between the dizzying polarities of anarcho-capitalism and fading memories of Soviet certainty. How would President Putin, the former KGB man newly installed in the Kremlin following the sudden resignation of Boris Yeltsin, play his hand with regard to the news media? Would he build upon Mikhail Gorbachev's commitment to free speech, enshrined in the Russian constitution? Or would he he seek tighter control?

Irina Lukyanova, a former newspaper journalist, was at that time presenter of the main political current affairs programme of SkaT, a television station in Samara, in the Volga. I asked her what influence she had over who appeared on her show. 'I am allowed to choose,' she replied, 'except for those who pay for their places.' Those who pay? 'Yes, there are usually a couple of seats for those who pay, mainly politicians or business people.' How much do they pay? 'About a thousand US dollars. The price is set by the advertising department.' A further indignity, she explained, was the role demanded of journalists like her during election periods by the powerful regional politicians who, along with business tycoons, had taken control of much of Russia's political life in the post-Soviet period. Journalists are pressured to work for the election campaign teams where, in a few weeks, they can earn as much as in the rest of the year. Around election time, Irina said she was required to act as 'interviewer' for what in effect were party-political broadcasts—a clear conflict of roles. She had dealt with this situation by developing a 'cold and mechanical' style of interviewing for these occasions, the stance of a 'microphone holder' rather than a journalist. I asked her to demonstrate, using a spoon as a microphone. It was an impressively coded statement against a practice she bitterly resented, but which she felt she could not change.

In the Russian newspaper world, life was tough in a different way. Alexander Yakhontov edited a weekly paper in a small city a few hundred miles south of Moscow. He made a start in journalism in 1991, during the warm spring which followed the ending of the Cold War. Like most papers, this one had begun life as a tiny cog in the Communist Party machine—the voice of the local Young Communist League. In its communist heyday, it recorded a meaningless but impressive-sounding circulation figure of 50,000. Reborn as a title owned by its staff with what Yakhontov styled a 'public watchdog' role in its community, the paper was struggling to sell 4,000 copies a week and had been subject to repeated bouts of harassment from the local governor. When I asked Alexander Yakhontov about his hopes for the future, he replied: 'The intelligentsia needs independent opinion. I hope we shall survive, despite all the hardships.'

During that same trip, I revisited the huge Ostankino broadcasting complex on the edge of Moscow to meet people at the centre of the battle for control of the by now partially privatized Russian television system. Here the Kremlin was still fixing television industry politics at the highest level, doing battle with a range of new media barons or 'oligarchs', whose fortunes had typically been amassed during Yeltsin-era privatizations.

It was a murky atmosphere, yet I was struck by the contrast between what I saw in the NTV news production suite that evening and what I had observed 14 years earlier, when I had visited Ostankino as the head of a BBC News delegation just before the fall of the Berlin Wall. That day, arriving at about 11 am, I was asked whether I would like to observe the rehearsals for that evening's main television news bulletin, which was to be read by a thickset man in a shiny suit. 'How can you rehearse a bulletin so long before it goes on air, since you can't yet know what the main news items will be?' I enquired. 'We already have our script. It has been cleared,' my host replied. In Soviet Russia, breaking news conformed to the working patterns of bureaucrats.

Fourteen years later, NTV's evening news led with a reheated allegation of Kremlin involvement in the bombing of a Moscow apartment block, used to justify escalation of the war in Chechnya. This war, between the Russian state and a separatist movement, threatened emerging media freedoms in Russia, exemplified when Russian troops handed over Andrei Babitsky, a Russian journalist working for the US government-funded Radio Liberty, to rebel troops. President Putin had described Babitsky's reporting as 'much more dangerous than firing a machine gun'. As I entered the NTV newsroom, the first computer screen I saw displayed the Drudge Report, the American muck-raking Internet site. That same day, revelations about sexual misdemeanours by an executive involved in a corporate TV row would appear on a Russian website specializing in what Russians call 'compromat': sleaze. This was no utopia of free expression, but it illuminated a turbulent post-Cold War media world very distant from the old *Pravda*, with its global network of dull writers trained to eat well and service the party line.

Putin's guard dogs

Looking back at this snapshot in time, with President Putin now in his third term of office, it is clear that the grip of the Russian state has been retightened. Russia's constitutional guarantee of press freedom still stands, though it has been formally qualified with regard to terrorism and 'threats to the state'. Russia is also one of the most dangerous places in the world for journalists, as we were reminded when Anna Politkovskaya, a journalist for *Novaya Gazeta*, was shot dead near her home on Putin's birthday; 7 October 2006. Two years earlier, in 2004, she had written that 'we are hurtling back into a Soviet abyss, into an information vacuum that spells death from our own ignorance. All we have left is the Internet, where information is still freely available. For the rest, if you want to go on working as a journalist, it's total servility to Putin. Otherwise it can be death, the bullet, poison, or trial—whatever our special services, Putin's guard dogs, see fit.'

Russian television has, in effect, been taken back under state control, whether directly or indirectly via investments from business organizations close to the Kremlin. Freedom House considers Russia's news media firmly in the 'not free' category—a judgement, say critics of the American organization, which merely reflects its long-standing prejudice.

Scholars offer a more subtle picture: 'conflicting signals' in the words of one assessment, which mentions an enriched culture of television entertainment and a bustling press, whilst acknowledging firm control of broadcast news media and the use of the courts to harass journalists. These Russia watchers see change happening through the medium of the Internet, which, President Putin himself has repeatedly stated, will remain uncontrolled by the state. Ivan Zassoursky, a journalist (or these days a Russian 'hackademic', given his position with Moscow State University) makes this judgement:

> The new Russian Empire seems to me like an iceberg melting in the Internet. A global information environment slowly but surely becomes the medium of choice for the new generation, bringing with it new possibilities, new habits and even new values, putting in place new rules of the game, which over time may trigger the next stage of evolution to unfold society-wide, as has already happened to the information-rich elite of the country.

China—the adaptive state

But why should Putin's Russia look to a liberal model with regard to the Internet at a time when authoritarian regimes elsewhere, such as Saudi Arabia or, most tellingly, China, appear to be successfully managing their own, more controlled version of the Internet? Beijing's response has been decisive, building its own online infrastructure and superstructure, designed to replicate most of the features of the global Internet, but in a manner which reserves to the Chinese Communist Party high levels of control.

As long ago as 1995 China inaugurated its famous Great Firewall of China, designed to keep out undesirable foreign service providers, followed by its Golden Shield system, designed to suppress any activity which threatens the country's political leadership or the state's proclaimed goal of 'harmony'. So Chinese web users use Baidu rather than Google, Renren rather than Facebook, and Weibo rather than Twitter. According to Gady Epstein of *The Economist*, 'the Party has achieved something few had thought possible: the construction of a distinct national Internet'. This, he adds, 'resembles a fenced-off playground with paternalistic guards'. The guards, numbering perhaps as many as 100,000, engage in a wide variety of techniques, ranging from 'deep packet inspection' of online traffic to deployment of bloggers and microbloggers to feed the web with harmony-inducing content. These relatively soft powers are backed by heavier methods, including long jail sentences, to deal with significant dissenters like Liu Xiaobo, a writer sentenced in 2009 to 11 years for his part in an online manifesto calling for an end to authoritarian rule.

There is no doubt that this Chinese Internet, with over 560 million users, is massive, messy, and dynamic, supporting a huge e-commerce market and facilitating a level of public or semi-public conversation which has not previously existed in China and which has, on a number of occasions, resulted in strong action against

3. In 1989, protest in Beijing's Tiananmen Square led to a fierce crackdown by the Chinese authorities. This televised image of a lone, unidentified man in front of a tank stands as testament. In the Internet era, the Chinese authorities pursue a more subtle route to controlling news

lower-level or regional officials (see Figure 3). In Epstein's view, China's 'adaptive state' is providing a level of news media and Internet freedom designed to support a growing sense of economic well-being, which is itself the most reliable defence against radical threats to the Party's leadership.

For Chinese journalists, this creates an operating environment in which they can pursue stories with an enhanced sense of independence and feel that they are holding at least some agents of power to account. Conversation online is human, sardonic, witty, and grumbling rather than regimented. When you meet and talk to Chinese newspaper and magazine journalists, they are lively and critical conversationalists, though in official situations they exhibit caution. Thousands are being educated in America and Europe. Newspapers and magazines have, in recent years, been encouraged to fund themselves increasingly through advertisements, encouraging competition for audience attention.

China's approach to journalism and the online world is certainly being watched closely by smaller states in Asia and Africa, where Chinese economic influence is also strong. A United Nations conference on telecommunications governance in December 2012 exposed a clear divide between America, Europe, and other developed countries, who argue for Internet freedom, and China, Russia, Saudi Arabia, Nigeria, Vietnam, Sudan, and others, who want to set their own terms for the way the Internet works in their own countries—a direction of travel which some fear will lead to a fragmented 'Splinternet'. In a vote, 89 states supported a move to recognize every state's sovereign right to connect to the Internet in its own way.

From Velvet Revolution to the Arab Spring

This is all a very long way from the polarities of a post-Cold War triumph for the principles of liberal, democratic Western journalistic values. In the wave of political change which swept through Eastern Europe following the collapse of the Berlin Wall, 17 states were hurled from the edge of the Soviet empire towards the accession lounge of a European Union committed to free news media. Article 11 of the EU Charter of Fundamental Rights states: 'Everyone has the right to freedom of expression... without interference by public authority and regardless of frontiers. The freedom and pluralism of the media shall be respected.' In practice, some of these new members of the EU, such as Romania (joined 2007) and even Hungary (joined 2004), have struggled at times to demonstrate an unequivocal commitment to these principles, as indeed have older members of the EU, including Greece and Italy.

Even more complex has been the wave of political change in the Middle East labelled at its outset in 2010 'the Arab Spring', which brought the fall of dictatorships in Tunisia, Libya, Egypt, and Yemen, driven in part by a new social media activism connected to mainstream providers of local and international news. Although often likened in Western media coverage to previous populist surges towards democracy, these uprisings have also involved other potent forces, among them radical forms of political Islam. Joseph Massad, a Jordan-born Palestinian academic, told Al Jazeera that the term Arab Spring was itself 'part of a US strategy of controlling [the movement's] aims and goals'. An analysis of Egyptian news media by Naomi Sakr, two years after the first uprising, says that journalistic 'practitioners struggled to define the different but overlapping codes and rationales of activism, citizen journalism and professional journalism'. When the fall of the Mubarak regime was followed by the army's ousting of his elected successor, President Morsi, long-standing rigidities in a state-dominated media system still persisted, leading Sakr to idenitify a paradox that 'journalism nearly two years after the revolutionary uprising looked little different from what went before...yet changes in many areas of journalism practice were too fundamental to be undone'. It remains to be seen whether the Egyptian state will find its way towards support for the legal protection of free and independent journalism of the kind that Sakr and numerous others have demanded.

American angst

If a glance around Russia, China, and the Middle East calls into question the narrative of unchecked momentum towards free news media and liberal, democratic values, so too does recent debate about journalism in the United States itself. By 2010, Robert McChesney, the US media scholar, was proclaiming in the United States nothing less than 'a stunning collapse of journalism as it has been known for the past century, if not the nation's entire history'.

This apocalyptic pessimism has diverse roots. One influential strand, argued from the political left and most famously set out by the linguist Noam Chomsky and his collaborator Edward Herman, states that Western media structures are best understood as part of a 'propaganda model', which harnesses their activities to the purposes and values of established power structures in politics and business. Chomsky himself has likened the *New York Times* to the pre-1989 *Pravda*, and his followers dismiss the BBC as an agent of government propaganda.

A second strand, focused upon cultural issues, questions whether media companies whose businesses are focused primarily upon the pursuit of large audiences through entertainment in order to boost their advertising can be reliable protectors of the high civic goals of the free press, as understood in the First Amendment to the American constitution. Neil Postman's book *Amusing Ourselves to Death* made the case that television was simply incapable of providing the kind of serious news required in a successful democracy. James Fallows's *Breaking the News: How the Media Undermine American Democracy* developed the case against the drift towards 'infotainment'. A group calling itself 'concerned journalists' emerged to advocate a 'public journalism' committed to robust professional standards of accurate and balanced reporting and issued a manifesto which stated: 'The First Amendment—that a free press is an independent institution—is threatened for the first time in our history without government meddling. In this world, the First Amendment becomes a property right establishing ground rules for free economic competition, not free speech. This is a fundamental and epic change with enormous implications for democratic society.' These debates continue to strike chords in media systems at an earlier stage of development, such as those in India and Pakistan or Kenya and South Africa.

In Europe, despite a prevailing ethos of state investment in broadcast news, intellectuals from the left and the right have also delivered strong critiques of the news media landscape, accusing politicians of lacking the courage to take on excessive concentrations of media power. The French sociologist Pierre Bourdieu's famous study of television journalism found a system where 'all production is oriented toward preserving established values' and where competition 'rather than generating originality and diversity, tends to favour uniformity'.

In Italy, Silvio Berlusconi, prime minister for nine years, commanded patronage in the state broadcasting system, RAI, whilst simultaneously enjoying his position as a dominant figure in Italy's largest commercial television group, Mediaset. Václav Havel, dramatist, hero of Czechoslovakia's Velvet Revolution in 1989, and subsequently president of the Czech Republic, chose World Press Freedom Day in 2002 to issue this warning: 'In a situation where there will be no direct political oppression and censorship, there might be more complex issues, especially at the economic level, that may affect freedom of speech. Italy might represent an early form of this problem.'

Convergent media, convergent regulators

The core charge of most of these critiques of the Western news media is that their corporate owners are too powerful and too influential politically, in a democratic system where political parties need wealthy backers. More fundamentally, these media giants are driven by the expectations of financial markets, which creates tension with their civic or communal responsibilities as news providers. In the United States especially, corporate ownership structures continuously shift in a way that makes them difficult to follow. So, in 2013, ABC was a subsidiary of the Walt Disney Company. CBS had in the previous decade been owned by Westinghouse, best known as a power generation company, by Viacom, and then controlled by Sumner Redstone's National Amusements group. NBC was owned for several years by General Electric or GE, a vast industrial group with interests ranging from power generation to aerospace and which for a time worked in partnership with Vivendi, a French telecommunications company. But in 2013, GE offloaded its media assets to the cable TV company Comcast, leaving the Comcast subsidiary, NBC Universal, with interests in television, film, and theme parks.

Faced with such restless manoeuvres and 'market failures', politicians feel pressure to support regulation, designed to protect media plurality and ensure high standards, along with investment in non-commercial media such as public service broadcasting in order to provide a balanced mix of services. Arguments of this kind have prevailed in most parts of the world, except in the United States, where they are associated with the politics of the left, Washington-centred political power, and disregard for the First Amendment. Consequently, regulation of broadcasting, including broadcast news, is a near-universal phenomenon. Newspapers, however, are for the most part regulated, if at all, only through voluntary arrangements which do not involve the power of statute. In the UK, the 2011 Leveson Report controversially recommended 'statutory underpinning' for a new press regulator and so ran into implacable opposition from newspaper publishers.

American broadcast regulation is, in practice, chiefly concerned with issues of competition. In recent years, the Federal Communications Commission has steered clear of attempts to draw it into regulation of content. In Europe, regulation on both broadcast content and issues of competition are framed by EU law, and national and European regulatory structures have been changed to recognize the overlaps between regulation of telecommunications, broadcasting structures, and content. The UK's converged regulator (created in 2003) is Ofcom, the Office of Communications. It deals with the full spread of economic, technological, and content issues, though its remit has never been formally extended to matters concerning the development of the Internet. European and American regulators meanwhile seek to base their judgements on the principle of 'net neutrality', which asserts that providers of telecoms networks should not discriminate against particular types of online traffic, so ensuring an 'open' or 'end-to-end' Internet. This is territory where regulatory thinking is certain to be tested further in the coming years.

What do these complex activities mean for journalism? They tell us that the news industry has in the last two decades moved from being a substantial industry in its own right, with a strong and distinctive industrial and professional culture, to one now occupying an important but quite small space as a particular type of media 'content', set in a world of corporate media ambition, telecommunications regulation, and global Internet governance. No wonder journalists feel that the earth has moved.

Chapter 3
The first casualty: journalists at war

'The first casualty when war comes is truth,' said Senator Hiram Johnson in 1917, a provocation to journalists about their vulnerability to patriotic pressure that has echoed down the century, from an age of relative innocence in the politics of mass media, to a digital era which is transforming both war reporting and the nature of war itself.

According to Philip Knightley's account of war reporting, *The First Casualty*, it should only be in a 'war of national survival', such as the Second World War, that journalists entertain the idea of explicit cooperation with the state and its propaganda. Knightley goes on to argue that journalists in modern times have grown so dependent upon the military authorities for access and information that it has become more or less impossible to do an honest and independent job as a war reporter. 'The age of the war correspondent as hero is clearly over,' he declares.

In the final decade of the last century and the first decade of the current one, events began to cloud these judgements. In a post-Cold War, nuclear-armed world more vulnerable to insurgency and terrorism than wars of explicit territorial ambition, warfare has also been changed by the same digital communications technologies which have shaken up the media; from visual data analytics, cyber surveillance and helmet-mounted video cameras to the robotic weapons known as 'drones'. General Sir Rupert Smith, commander of UN forces in the Bosnian wars of the 1990s, in his book *The Utility of Force*, describes a shift from 'industrial war', with relatively clear 'rules' and boundaries, to 'war among the people', where boundaries in space and in time can appear non-existent. The civil war in Syria, implacable at the time of writing, provides a grim example of 'war among the people'. In the Syrian war, not only did many journalists lose their lives, but for long periods large sections of the country became no-go areas for journalists. In these circumstances, news supply polarizes between the suspect propaganda of external powers and the online pictures, audio, and text, from activists and bystanders, circulating on social media networks. In such a media environment 'truth' becomes even harder to verify or deny.

From Vietnam to the Balkan wars

From a military perspective, it has always been obvious that news media activity is there to be managed to the maximum extent possible. In wars where journalists break free, the generals risked losing the battle for hearts and minds. The Vietnam War was widely judged to have been lost on television and it is no coincidence that the photographic legacy of this war is so rich. Eddie Adams's famous picture of a street execution (see Figure 4) sticks firmly in my own visual memory; as troubling in its rawness as Goya's famous depiction of a French firing squad gunning down members of the Spanish resistance in May 1808. Here, the truth-telling photographer and artist are literally on the front line.

When Britain went to war with Argentina in 1982 over the latter's incursions into the colonial outpost of the Falkland Islands, the lessons of Vietnam had been fully taken on board by the authorities. The only way journalists could get to this war or transmit stories from it was with the aid of the Royal Navy. The renowned war photographer, Don McCullin, whose work from Vietnam had been acclaimed, was not allowed on the ship

4. The Vietnam War was said to have been won and lost on television, but it also generated powerful still images, like this one by photographer Eddie Adams

carrying journalists to the South Atlantic. This anachronistic conflict stands as one of the last when journalists from warring countries were successfully confined behind their own lines and controlled in such detail by the military authorities.

In the 1990s, the availability of new communications technologies in a series of conflicts in the Arabian Gulf and later in the Balkans turned the world of the war reporter upside down. In the first Gulf War (1990–1), the American military authorities, mindful of Vietnam, operated strict censorship and control of reporter 'pools', but this did not prevent the ten-year-old Cable News Network (CNN), along with other American and UK broadcasters and newspaper reporters, operating behind enemy lines in Baghdad, from where they were able to contribute unforgettable accounts of smart missiles navigating their way towards targets, along with civilian carnage. Media coverage of this short war, over in less than a year, also made extensive use of video provided by the military itself, drawing criticism for the way it was used to offer viewers what some saw as an arcade game-style experience rather than a sober account of events. Ted Koppel, presenter of the ABC show *Nightline*, spoke for many journalists when he said: 'I'm not sure the public's interest is served by seeing what seems to have been such a painless war, when 50,000 to 100,000 people may have died on the other side.'

The 'Balkan wars', which raged through Yugoslavia during the 1990s, recast the borders of the European Union from pieces that had once sat within the Soviet empire. These were interrelated ethnic and national conflicts, in which the global powers at first attempted to avoid direct involvement, but which by 1999 had drawn NATO, led by President Clinton and his close ally UK prime minister Tony Blair, into a bombing campaign which quickly yielded a UN-led peace and reconstruction process. It was in these conflicts, on the eastern edge of Europe, that the news media and the military started to understand the extent to which digital media were reshaping the craft of war reporting.

Prior to the first wave of bombing, NATO's military leaders showed every sign that they anticipated an unchanged world, where they could control information and the movements of journalists around fixed media schedules. What they found themselves dealing with was a 24-hour television news cycle and a dissolution of geographic media boundaries, which enabled Western news reports to be sourced from Serbian broadcasters' cameras. NATO commanders brought in 'spin doctors' and simultaneously targeted the offending TV stations, dealing another blow to the vanishing convention that journalists enjoy neutral status in international conflicts.

The Yugoslav wars also showed, however, that in the digital age it was very difficult for military leaders to destroy unhelpful news media. The dissident Belgrade radio station B92, a source of irritation to the Belgrade authorities from its inception, was shut down numerous times, but never successfully taken off air once it mastered the art of reaching audiences via the Internet. Today, B92 is a major player in the Serbian market for commercial television, entertainment, and sport.

Global online media also offered easy chat across enemy lines. I recall sitting in a barber's shop in London during the early days of the allied bombardment of Belgrade and being taken aback to hear, on a television phone-in, people speaking 'live' from towns and cities under bombardment from 'our' aircraft. Meanwhile, the BBC News website, at the time the most visited in Europe, offered hyperlinks to sites devoted to distributing information and propaganda on behalf of the Serb 'enemy' authorities. As General Wesley Clark later commented, 'in future, all wars will be fought on the assumption that the news media operate behind enemy lines'.

A number of other conflicting lessons of media warcraft emerged from these conflicts. One, strongly visible in the rear-view mirror provided by the War Crimes trials in The Hague which followed the peace settlement, drew attention to the paradox that in a rapidly globalizing, online media ecology, there was still a role for more traditional local and national news media, which in the Balkans underpinned the political ideologies that contributed to the conflict.

Another paradox was the way that 'wars among the people' could escape the attention of the news media. Even on the day that NATO bombers attacked Yugoslavia, on 24 March 1999, the first NATO action on European soil since the end of the Second World War, only one British newspaper, the *Daily Telegraph*, thought the news justified clearing its front page. The others all reported events prominently, but also felt they had to reassure readers with other diversions. *The Times* obliged with a page-one trail for a feature on the writer Bruce Chatwin's love affair with style guru Jasper Conran. The *Guardian*'s preferred distraction was

'Doctors—the new fertility gods', and the *Independent*'s an item on England football managers. In the week prior to the bombing, the proportion of each paper's space given to foreign news ranged between 8 and 12 per cent for the broadsheets and between 0 and 4 per cent for the tabloids. Wars among the people have a way of settling into the background, rather than commanding regular and high-profile attention.

Controversy about a different sort of detachment arises from the strange case of the Independent Television News libel action, which resulted from its reporting in 1992 of a Serbian-run camp in Trnopolje in Bosnia. One still image from this footage, showing an emaciated man behind barbed wire, was splashed by newspapers as evidence of a Serbian 'Belsen 1992'. Five years later, the picture was on the cover of a small, left-wing magazine, *LM* (formerly *Living Marxism*), with the accusation that it had 'fooled the world' by emotively misrepresenting the plight of Trnopolje's inmates. One target of *LM*'s campaign was the concept of 'journalism of attachment', coined from the Bosnian war zone by one of the BBC's most celebrated foreign correspondents, Martin Bell. This approach, says Bell, is consistent with the goals and rules of journalistic objectivity as truth-telling, offering 'journalism that cares as well as knows'. The London libel courts ruled in favour of ITN and *LM* went out of business in March 2000.

Journalism that cares as well as knows was one answer to the troubling problem of retaining audience interest in international affairs. In the period from 1970 to 2000, the average news soundbite on American television was cut from 42 seconds to 8 seconds, as news shows battled to hold viewers' attention. Sometimes wars were so long, as with the dreary, routine bombardment of Northern Iraq in the late 1990s, that they were barely reported in the Western media. Many Americans were, no doubt, astonished to be told in 2002, as President George W. Bush talked up the idea of a decisive war against Iraq, that the First Gulf War had never, entirely, ended.

The 'war' on terror

Another decisive shift in the nature of war reporting was precipitated by the al-Qaeda terrorist attacks on Manhattan and Washington on 11 September 2001 (9/11). In the minutes immediately following, newscaster Tom Brokaw announced that 'terrorists have declared war', a media framing adopted or intuitively agreed in newspaper banner headlines around the world: 'Krieg Gegen Amerika' (Berlin's *Grosste Zeitung*) or 'War on America' (UK's *Daily Telegraph*). Nine days later, President George W. Bush officially declared a 'War on Terror' (see Figure 5).

This language was and remains controversial. A former head of British intelligence has insisted that 9/11 is properly seen as a crime, not an act of war, and during the presidency of Barack Obama the term 'war on terror' was officially displaced by the bureaucratese of 'Overseas Contingency Operation'. These formulations have legal significance—for example, determining whether individuals apprehended in conflicts are entitled to rights under the Geneva Convention. They also have obvious media significance, indicating the onset of a struggle against forces so generalized as to exclude the possibility of the geographic and time boundaries which framed warfare in previous centuries.

Anthony Giddens, the sociologist, has spoken of an era of 'states without enemies' and 'enemies without states'. Mary Kaldor has noted a striking shift over the course of the last century from warfare which killed eight military people for every civilian to an inversion of that ratio: 1:8 by the year 2000. Kaldor proposes the term 'new war' whilst other scholars speak of 'diffuse war', to identify a phenomenon which extends to the types of conflict that occurred in Rwanda, Darfur, and Sri Lanka, where television coverage of warfare which did not directly involve major Western powers was either late or spasmodic.

The Daily Telegraph

www.telegraph.co.uk — Britain's biggest-selling quality daily — Wednesday, September 12, 2001 50p

War on America

Inside
Weather page 9
TV & Radio pages 22 & 23
Business pages 24-27
Sport pages 29-32

THE United States was on a war footing last night after the most devastating terrorist attack in history.

Two hijacked passenger airliners crashed into the twin towers of New York's World Trade Centre. Both towers collapsed with the loss of thousands of lives, sending out great clouds of thick dust that covered buildings and people in the streets like volcanic ash. Lower Manhattan was evacuated and the New York skyline changed for ever.

Minutes later in Washington DC a third hijacked aircraft crashed into the Pentagon, the heart of America's military machine. A fourth, believed to be heading for the presidential retreat Camp David, crashed near Pittsburgh.

The atrocity was meticulous in its co-ordination and horrifying in its effect.

A global television audience watched in disbelief as live footage showed the second plane hitting the Trade Centre minutes after the first.

Land borders were closed and airspace cleared of all but military aircraft as US forces were put on "high alert".

Financial centres were paralysed when Wall Street closed and shares plunged across world markets. The departments of Justice, State, Treasury, Defence and the CIA were all evacuated.

President Bush was flown to a bunker in Nebraska before returning to the White House. He pledged: "Make no mistake, we will hunt down and punish those responsible for these cowardly acts."

Reports: Pages 2, 3, 4, 5, 6, 7, 8, 9 and eight-page supplement. Comment: Pages 18 & 19

5. The world's media were quick to label the terrorist attacks of 9/11 as 'war'. It would turn out to be much more complicated than that

Post 9/11, the West's military opponents were elusive. The perpetrators of the specific 9/11 mass murder (3,000 died) were themselves the martyred dead. Their 'leader' or inspiration, Osama Bin Laden, was the 'head' of al-Qaeda: the most important figure in a loosely organized network which was not, in any conventional military sense, controlled by him. Nor had Bin Laden declared war on the United States. He was supposedly based in Afghanistan; the hunt for him would not end until 2011, when American special forces landed by his secret residential compound in Pakistan and shot him dead. Bin Laden's body was buried at sea at an undisclosed location.

In the decade between 9/11 and the death of Osama Bin Laden, the United States and its allies were permanently at war, first in Afghanistan, where a US-led coalition of forces ousted the Taliban government and then conducted an exhausting engagement with tribal forces supportive of the deposed Islamic fundamentalists. The Taliban conducted operations in the manner of an insurgency, their weapon of choice the 'improvised explosive device'.

In 2003, a US-led coalition invaded Iraq, where Sadam Hussain was accused of harbouring weapons of mass destruction, with a spectacular opening phase designed to 'shock and awe' the enemy. Research suggested that many Americans believed Sadam had been responsible for 9/11. Six weeks later, the coalition took Baghdad, inaugurating a much longer 'post-war' period in which insurgents violently disrupted the new, coalition-supported Iraqi government. A decade after the invasion, casualty levels in Iraq were as high as they had been during the official 'war'. Strikes by drones successfully targeted alleged terrorist group leaders in Pakistan and elsewhere, but also quite frequently slaughtered civilians. Were journalists in these environments still properly described as 'war correspondents'?

The Afghan and the Iraq wars had in common a sharp switch from conventional military operation to insurgency and counter-insurgency. In the phase of conventional war, reporters were offered positions 'embedded' with troops, ensuring a level of military control but offering 'a bargain' to news organizations able to place their reporters and camera operators closer to the front line. Critics said these 'embeds' (or, to their critics, 'in-beds') would be unable to speak freely like the 'independents', who were often far away from front-line military action. A post-war analysis conducted by Cardiff University concluded that embeds provided 'a useful addition to the mix' of war reporting, but that their operation was associated with 'a greater disregard for the welfare of independent journalists, particularly by US forces'.

By 2003, when the post-invasion phase of operations in Iraq began, online social media were changing in more fundamental ways the means by which information was gathered and distributed, in some cases challenging the accuracy of reports from established journalists, who often lacked access to anything more than official military sources. Weblogging or 'blogging' was by now an established form for the expression of opinion and the collaborative construction of news. Within three years, the microblogging site Twitter would add another dimension. Al-Qaeda's supporters were themselves expert in their use of social media, using the new networks to operate below the radar of official 'Big Media'.

Soon there was a set of blogs known as 'warblogs', taking a range of views about the conflict in Iraq, including from voices inside the besieged city. One of these, the work of an anonymous young architect, was published under the name Salam Pax, and became widely followed by mainstream news media. Professional news correspondents started to experiment with blogs as a further channel of immediate reporting, offering new range to the work of broadcast reporters. Christopher Allbritton set himself up as an independent war blogger in Iraqi Kurdistan, having raised money through his network on the Internet, in an unusual manifestation of 'crowdfunding'.

It was not long before military communications experts, desperate to win the social media war against al-Qaeda, began first to sanction and then to encourage blogging by serving soldiers. The Internet thus established itself as a primary site for competitive reporting of the Iraq War and its aftermath. From the authorities' point of view, there were bound to be risks in amassing daily troves of military video and in sanctioning the culture of the Internet within the armed forces: in 2010 a young American soldier, Chelsea (previously Bradley) Manning, leaked 750,000 documents and military video shot in Iraq and Afghanistan to the WikiLeaks whistleblower website.

If this was confusing for military and political leaders, it was not straightforward for professional journalists. During the opening phase of the Iraq War, as if in homage to Senator Hiram Johnson, American television presenters wore patriotic badges in their lapels, and NBC News's corporate symbol of the peacock acquired a stars and stripes embellishment. When the *New York Times* devoted space for many weeks to an acclaimed series of stories about the victims of Ground Zero, some wondered whether it was possible for even such an illustrious newspaper to maintain a detached and critical eye on the course of American foreign policy.

In the UK, the biggest media drama came in the war's aftermath, when a partially erroneous BBC radio report accused the government of 'sexing up' evidence used to justify the war. This precipitated a judicial inquiry whose final report (the Hutton Report) was widely dismissed as a whitewash, but which led to the resignation of the two most senior figures at the corporation, the director general, Greg Dyke, and the chairman, Gavyn Davies.

Al Jazeera and the Arab Street

For one news organization, however, the conflicts in Iraq, Afghanistan, and, soon, elsewhere in the Middle East presented a breakthrough opportunity. Al Jazeera, established in 1996 from the foundations of a BBC Arabic-language television service, is financed by the Emir of Qatar from a base in Doha and is believed to be the most watched television channel among 300 million Arabs living in 22 countries around the world. Al Jazeera, which also broadcasts in English, is one of a number of news channels presenting a challenge to the previous global domination of English-language television news services by the likes of the BBC and the big American players. It has, according to Nadim Shehadi of the Centre for Lebanese Studies in Oxford, 'had an impact on the whole of the media in the region. The others are forced to catch up and compete—even the printed media. There's a lot more freedom now, because there's no point in controlling information if you know that people are going to find out from somewhere else.'

By 2002, Al Jazeera had a staff of 350 journalists, including 50 foreign correspondents in 31 countries, serving an estimated audience of 35 million. Ten years later, the audience was said to be in excess of 50 million, though reliable statistics do not exist. Its executives insist that it has imbibed its values of impartial reporting from the BBC and the America of Ed Murrow, though its practice of describing Palestinian suicide bombers as 'martyrs' is widely considered a departure from those standards, as is its lack of curiosity about some of the stories closest to its home base in Doha. Provoked by Al Jazeera's success, the US Congress dug deep to fund a sickly pro-American rival, Al Hurra. More significant was the launch in 2003 of Al Arabiya, part of a profitable group of Arab entertainment channels, based in Dubai and supported by the conservative Saudis. During the first wave of protests which marked the start of the Arab Spring in January 2011, the *New York Times* commented that the protests 'have one thread uniting them: Al Jazeera... whose aggressive coverage has helped propel insurgent emotions from one capital to the next'.

Controversial in its earliest days as the preferred vehicle used by al-Qaeda for the release of its propaganda videos, Al Jazeera has acquired passionate enemies as well as friends. Coalition forces bombed its offices in Kabul and Baghdad, and Arab governments in Baghdad and Egypt have at various times closed down its offices and expelled its journalists. Al Jazeera's critics accuse it of pro-Sunni bias and (in its Arabic service) sustained anti-Semitism. But by 2013, Al Jazeera had acquired the scale, confidence, and cash to take on the American news media on their own turf, launching Al Jazeera America, with 900 journalists in 12 states, having bought Current TV, a failing current affairs channel led by former vice president Al Gore (Figure 6). The launch rhetoric of the new channel intruded ostentatiously into American soul searching about the challenges facing the country's own broadcast news media, by promising 'less opinion, less yelling and fewer celebrity sightings. We are not infotainment. We are in-depth and informative.' In a speech in 2011, Wadah Khanfar, director general of Al Jazeera from 2006 to 2011, gave his own account of the organization's creed, speaking of Al Jazeera's 'spiritual link with the masses' as the foundation of its mission. By this time, Al Jazeera faced a growing wave of competition, from long-established players like the BBC, but also from newer players like Russia Today, France 24, CCTV9 (China), and Iran's Press TV.

The complex, global news ecology in which war and conflict reporting occurs today has led media scholar Simon Cottle to speak of 'mediatized war', where the media dimensions of warlike acts are planned with the same attention to detail as other military logistics. Even the most provisional of protagonists show a level of media awareness unimaginable in the Vietnam era, as when a fighter in the wave of terrorist attacks on Mumbai in 2008 paused to make a mobile phone call direct to India TV.

War is further 'mediatized' by the continuous availability of old as well as new images from conflicts. This viewable, reviewable, and debatable material creates new forms of media activity as it is shared and discussed around the world. An example is the video

6. Al Jazeera, the Qatar-based broadcaster, successfully challenged the dominance of English-language TV news, expanding into the United States

record of the hanging of Saddam Hussain, which sits on the Internet in its 'official' version: designed to portray order and grave responsibility on behalf of the Iraqi authorities. Alongside it are other versions captured on mobile phones, in which a small assembled mob taunts the deposed Iraqi leader and provokes him into argument, even as the noose is tightened around his neck. This controversial media content can be connected online to countless other items, from the infamous 'home snaps' of Iraqi prisoners being tortured in the Abu Ghraib jail to the grandiosely misjudged 'Mission Accomplished' presidential ceremony on board USS *Abraham Lincoln*. Following Edward Snowden's leaking of information from the US National Security Agency in 2013, it is also now very clear that just as global social media are vital to the logistics and propaganda efforts of dispersed terrorist networks, so they are vital to the authorities seeking to disrupt them.

Chapter 4
Star-struck: journalism as entertainment

Journalism has always entertained as well as informed. Had it not done so, it would not have reached a mass audience. But in recent years, say journalism's critics, the instinct to amuse has driven out the will, and depleted the resource, for serious reporting and analysis.

Across the world, newspapers and magazines have piled into this infotainment mêlée, competing for columns written in the name of the latest celebrity chef or sports star. For a period, the highest-paid writer in British newspapers was an astrologist, Jonathan Cainer. Infotainment is popular everywhere, but surveys over the years have confirmed that the bug has bitten deepest in the United States and the UK. A 2013 study of digital news trends for the Reuters Institute for the Study of Journalism found that UK audiences, especially young females, had the biggest appetite for celebrity stories, considerably more so than news audiences in Germany or France.

At its most commercially self-generating, the celebrity system is able to invent its own stars through specially concocted media events. 'Reality television' shows, like *Survivor*, *Big Brother*, and *I'm a Celebrity... Get Me Out of Here* or 'live' talent competitions, produce instant celebrities, who can be interviewed on daytime TV and featured in magazines and newspapers. Often this alternative 'reality' appears to obliterate other realities. As the American satirical magazine and website *The Onion* put it in a headline just a month after the 11 September attacks on Manhattan and Washington: 'Shattered Nation Longs to Care About Stupid Bullshit Again'.

To critics like Neil Postman, this is a prophecy triumphantly vindicated. Postman's book *Amusing Ourselves to Death* made the case that television is, by its nature, a medium of entertainment, and that as it displaces print as the primary medium of news, it is bound to result in a less informed public. 'Dumbing down' is the phrase frequently used to label this phenomenon. Television news, Postman says, 'is a format for entertainment, not for education, reflection or catharsis'. Yet this is no open-and-shut case. Television news is, especially in countries where it has been protected by regulation and/or benefited from sustained investment, regarded by most people as their most trusted source of news.

The tabloid instinct

The tension between the serious news instinct and entertainment certainly isn't new to journalism. When William Randolph Hearst launched his *New York Mirror* in 1924, he declared that the *Mirror* would provide '90 per cent entertainment, 10 per cent information—and the information without boring you'.

Strictly speaking, a tabloid is a newspaper page exactly half the size of a broadsheet page: a mathematical relationship which stems from the fact that publishers need to be able to print tabloid and broadsheet newspapers on the same presses. It is, in all sorts of ways, a misleading handle since most of the British tabloids which have given the term its contemporary meaning, the *Sun*, the *Daily Mail*, the *Daily Express*, and the *News of the World*, began life as broadsheets. In many countries, the most respectable newspapers have long been tabloids or tabloid variants, France's *Le Monde* and Spain's *El País* among them. Germany's *Bild-Zeitung*, tabloid in format and content, is Europe's best-selling newspaper.

Silvester Bolam, the *Daily Mirror*'s editor from 1948 to 1953, felt no need to apologize for a louder, brasher style of journalism, announcing on his first front page: 'The *Mirror* is a sensational newspaper. We make no apology for that. We believe in the sensational presentation of news and views ... as a necessary and valuable service in these days of mass readership and democratic responsibility.' Sensationalism, Bolam said on a later occasion, 'means the vivid and dramatic presentation of events so as to give them a forceful impact on the mind of the reader. It means big headlines, vigorous writing, simplification into familiar, everyday language, and wide use of illustration by cartoons and photographs.' By 1968, under the admired leadership of Hugh Cudlipp, the left-leaning *Mirror* sold 5.3 million copies a day, the most successful newspaper in the world.

The Murdoch factor

Just before that landmark, in 1964, Cudlipp launched a brand new title, the *Sun*, as a rebranded version of the trade unions' *Daily Herald*, but aimed at the aspirational tastes of 'a middle class couple aged 28 and living in Reading'. The paper failed to thrive and by 1969 was sold to the young Australian publisher Rupert Murdoch, who had already purchased the *News of the World*, the naughtiest of Britain's Sunday newspapers. Murdoch told staff that he wanted the *Sun* to focus on 'sex, sport and contests'. One of its trademarks would be the 'page three girl'—a daily photograph of a near-naked woman. By the time the *Sun* soared past the *Mirror* in 1978, Murdoch was buying newspapers in the United States, first in Texas, then, in 1976, the *New York Post*. In Britain, faced with a challenge from the *Daily Star*, Murdoch brought in a new editor, Kelvin Mackenzie, who combined an ability to stretch the limits of taste and journalistic ethics with a passionate loyalty to the newly elected prime minister Margaret Thatcher, whose backing Murdoch would need as he developed his UK television business.

When Margaret Thatcher led Britain to war against Argentina in 1982, Murdoch and Mackenzie were well into their stride. The *Sun*'s famous headline, 'Gotcha!', over the story of an Argentinian warship torpedoed by a British submarine, was a trademark offering from an editor alternately brilliant, boorish, and casual about the basic rules of journalism. During the Falklands War, the *Sun* published an 'interview' with the widow of a dead serviceman with whom the paper had never spoken. Later, and after a long period of defiance, it apologized for a front-page story headlined 'The Truth', which accused Liverpool football fans of urinating on rescue workers as they tried to save people in a stadium disaster in which 96 fans were crushed to death.

Sometimes Mackenzie's front pages were pure make-believe. There is no other explanation for the infamous 'Freddie Starr Ate My Hamster' in March 1986, referring to an obscure incident two years earlier, when the comedian pretended to eat a hamster in a sandwich as a joke. In the 1990s, the *Sun*'s star columnist, Richard Littlejohn, habitually concluded his ranting columns with the exasperated catchphrase 'You couldn't make it up.' But at the *Sun* you could and they did. Two decades later, these freebooting habits would prove costly to Murdoch's UK businesses when his *News of the World* was accused of phone hacking and other crimes, leading to the newspaper's closure and the establishment of the Leveson inquiry into the ethics, culture, and practices of the press.

Mackenzie's *Sun*, however, did not invent tabloid make-believe. The standard bearer in that regard was the *New York Enquirer*, which changed the course of tabloid history when in 1952, with a circulation of 17,000, it was bought by Generoso Pope, Jr.

The tabloid Pope

Pope, who knew and admired the *News of the World*, renamed his paper the *National Enquirer*, turned it tabloid and told his small team of journalists to concentrate on lurid crime. Fifteen years later, with a slew of competitors, the *Enquirer* was selling a million copies a week. By 1975, boosted by sales at supermarket checkouts, circulation hit five million. In 1978, an edition of the *Enquirer* featuring a photograph of the corpse of Elvis Presley sold seven million copies, a peak not since exceeded.

Like all good tabloids, Pope's *Enquirer* had moments of high political impact. It was the *Enquirer*'s photograph in 1988 of presidential candidate Gary Hart on board a yacht called *Monkey Business* with a young woman called Donna Rice that ended Hart's political career. But countless other stories were simply made up, such as: 'Hitler Seen Alive in US' or 'JFK Alive on Skorpios' (complete with picture) or 'Mom Cleans Kids by Putting Them in Clothes Washer'.

Bill Sloan, who worked on the *National Enquirer* and other tabloids, has explained how experienced writers and editors like himself 'were routinely able to shift gears between out-and-out trash and serious reportage. One day they were inventing bogus stories for *News Extra* or even grinding out soft-core porn for the *National Bulletin*... The next day, they were interviewing real people, writing legitimate articles, and striving mightily for documentation and credibility.' Sloan's explanation for the decline of tabloid circulations in the 1980s and 1990s is that by then all newspapers, along with most television, had muscled into tabloid territory. New genres in the tabloid spirit have included fictional columns, with comic or satirical purpose, and what its proponents call 'investigative comedy', exemplified by the clever and very funny satirical documentaries of American Michael Moore, ridiculing phenomena such as American gun culture.

Things do not look so funny, however, when high-profile mainstream journalism turns out to be infected with an easy-going relationship with facts. In 1996, a British documentary team working for Carlton Television faked sequences in a story about drug running in South America, for which the company was fined £2 million by the television industry regulator. In 1981, a young *Washington Post* reporter, Janet Cooke, was stripped of her Pulitzer Prize when it turned out that her award-winning story of child drug addiction was a work of imagination. Another newspaper columnist pretended to be suffering from cancer in order to make her column more engaging. Jayson Blair, a young black reporter on the *New York Times*, was exposed in 2003 as a serial faker of news stories, leading to his own resignation and that of two of the paper's most senior editors. Blair's later account of the scandal was tellingly entitled *Burning Down My Master's House*.

Celebrities squared

In the same way that journalism learned to make light of the boundary between fact and fiction, it has also become increasingly absorbed by the entertainment and sales potential of celebrity, with significant consequences for some journalistic practice.

In order to get pictures and stories about celebrities, journalists have to deal with an industry of agents and publicists, who make their own living from promoting the celebrity's brand through obtaining the 'right' media coverage. This is a strictly two-way commercial play, because the news media know that the right celebrity on a magazine cover, or star interview on a talk show, can boost audiences and draw in advertisers. So celebrity and its mediation are big money for everyone involved. It is inevitable that, in these circumstances, stories and pictures will be obtained not chiefly by the enterprise of reporters, but by organizations willing to pay the largest fees for some stories to dubious intermediaries.

Generoso Pope discovered the power of celebrity when, in 1969, the *National Enquirer* published a family photograph of the late President Kennedy, surrounded by a story headlined 'Jackie Blasted by Nurse who Brought up JFK's Children'. Sales of the *Enquirer* increased by almost a third, prompting Pope to dispatch the following instruction to his staff: 'I want her on the cover at least every couple of weeks.' This they did, often embellishing pictures with stories of the purest fiction, claiming Mrs Onassis had changed religion, allowed her children to grow marijuana at home, and turned her second husband's hair white.

Much the same phenomenon attended the tragic figure of Diana, Princess of Wales, who entered global media consciousness in September 1980 when she was identified as the likely bride of the heir to the British throne. During the fairy-tale phase of this story, the princess featured on page one of the *Sun* 16 times in a single month (see Figure 7). When she chose to appear on the BBC's flagship current affairs programme *Panorama*, in 1995, to discuss

7. Tabloid news feeds on celebrity: the controversial life and death of Princess Diana raised the temperature around issues of privacy and the paparazzi

the breakdown of her marriage, the programme had the biggest audience in its history. No wonder so many news photographers were on her tail as she sped into a Parisian underpass in August 1997 with a drunken chauffeur at the wheel.

At her funeral, the princess's brother famously accused the press of having his sister's 'blood on their hands', whilst on the other side of the Atlantic, the *National Enquirer* was pulping its latest edition headlined 'Di Goes Sex Mad: "I Can't Get Enough!"' Disgusted by press behaviour towards the princess, other celebrities, including Madonna, George Clooney, Tom Cruise, and Sylvester Stallone, called for stronger counter-attacks in the courts on the tabloids. But the trouble with the Diana affair, like so many other celebrity outrages, was that it turned out to involve an act of collaboration. In the late 1980s the *Sunday Times* was accused of printing lies about the troubled Charles and Diana relationship, based upon its expensive purchase of serialization rights to a book by Andrew Morton. It later turned out that Diana herself was Morton's primary source. This explains the fierce tensions which arose during the Leveson inquiry into the UK press in 2011–12, where a small group of celebrities, most prominently the actor Hugh Grant and the comedian Steve Coogan, became prominent supporters of the campaign for stronger regulation of the press through the 'Hacked Off' campaign. The newspapers, in return, sought to portray their celebrity opponents as wealthy toffs, out of touch with the concerns and interests of 'real' people.

Journalists as celebs

It is perhaps not surprising that some journalists who mix frequently with celebrities themselves become celebrities. Barbara Walters of ABC became the first million-dollar news presenter in the mid 1970s. Since then, the salaries of news presenters have multiplied and, like sports stars, actors, and models, some appear to be heavily concerned with maximizing the value of their brand, whether on the lecture circuit, opening supermarkets, hosting executive conferences, or even associating themselves with product sponsorship. News executives defend these arrangements by saying that the public is attracted by celebrity: this is what it takes to get people to pay attention to news.

Lavish spending on stars, however, has often been accompanied by sharp cuts in other even more expensive activities, such as newsgathering, especially overseas. Why would an American TV news service keep a well-informed but unglamorous foreign reporter in London, New York, Rome, or Tokyo if, when there's a big story, the audience 'wants to see' the star anchor live from the news scene? But anyone who knows anything about journalism will tell you that fly-in, fly-away stars are no substitute for reporters who know the terrain and who can make judgements based upon extensive off-air inquiry.

In these days of instant TV news, it is not unusual for an on-the-spot reporter to be handed electronically via head office the latest news he or she is supposed to be 'reporting', enabling the 'reporter' to stand in front of the camera with the appearance that he or she has just discovered the information. Another inevitable vice of celebrity television journalism is that it favours appearance more than journalistic acumen, a problem particularly destructive to the careers of older female presenters. Set this alongside the *Washington Post*'s desk book or guidelines on 'the reporter's role', which reads plaintively: 'Although it has become increasingly difficult for this newspaper and for the press generally to do so since Watergate, reporters should make every effort to remain in the audience, to be the stagehand rather than the star, to report the news, not to make the news.' Or note these comments by Richard Sambrook, a former director of BBC News, and now director of the Centre for Journalism at Cardiff University: 'On-screen talent, not content, is becoming the basis of difference between rival American news broadcasters and we are starting to see those same pressures in Britain.'

The tabloid decade

The case for good tabloid journalism is that it can and does widen access to politics and other serious subjects. The related case for tabloid magazine reporting, of the kind retailed so successfully by publications like *Hello!* and *OK!*, is that it is, at worst, harmless entertainment, and at best a prism through which readers can assess and discuss moral and lifestyle choices in an enjoyable way.

A related point is made with respect to a famous incident in the history of 'tabloid television', the coverage in the mid 1990s of the trial of O. J. Simpson, the black footballer accused of murdering his wife and a male friend. After the Simpson trial, Dan Lungren, California's attorney general, complained about the 'oprahization' of American juries—a reference to the heated debates and instant verdicts of shows like the one then hosted by Oprah Winfrey. 'Talk show watchers are widely considered by prosecutors and professional jury consultants to be more likely than others to distrust official accounts of "the truth",' Lungren said. Regrettable though this alleged tendency may be from the point of view of an attorney general, Lungren failed to acknowledge the risk of blemishes in 'official accounts of truth', not least in the minds of black people. In the words of Kevin Glynn, an academic commentator, tabloid media 'multiply and amplify the heterogenous voices and viewpoints in circulation in contemporary culture, giving rein to many that are typically excluded from the dominant regime of truth through the dynamics of race, class, gender, age and sexuality'. Catharine Lumby, an Australian journalist and academic, has gone further, arguing that shows like Winfrey's 'exemplify a new form of public speech, one which privileges experience over knowledge, emotion over reason, and popular opinion over expert advice'. David Kamp suggested in an article in *Vanity Fair* that 'the tabloidification of American life—of the news, of the culture, yea, of human behaviour—is such a sweeping phenomenon that it can't be dismissed as merely a jokey footnote to the history of the

1990s. Rather, it's the very hallmark of our times; if the decade must have a name... it might as well be the Tabloid Decade.'

Tabloids online

If the 1990s provided the tabloid decade, the first decade of the 21st century has certainly been the Online Decade, as the digital communications revolution made deep impacts upon every aspect of the news business. These issues are considered more roundly in the final chapter of this book, but here we ask: Does the diversity of online news media contain or feed the tabloid beast?

In the big debates around journalism in recent years, expressions of concern about infotainment and the trivialization of news have certainly become less prominent. For this, there are perhaps three explanations.

The first is that the Internet's disruption of business models, especially but not only in the newspaper sector, has become such a severe problem that it has crowded other narratives directed at 'the problem with journalism today'. A second explanation is that the growth of online media has raised new questions, such as risks to personal privacy and the accessibility to children of 'unsuitable' material. A third explanation is that the alleged consequences of tabloidization in television and newspapers appear to have stabilized. One indicator carefully followed over the years by the Pew Centre for People and the Press has been the ever-decreasing length of news items and the interviews and reporting packages that form their structure. In its 2013 'State of the Media' report, Pew finds that network television news 'seems to be a rock of stability', with only marginal erosion of these building blocks in recent years.

It is undeniable, however, that the Internet itself has proved a richly hospitable environment for tabloid content built around celebrities. The singer Lady Gaga, with over 40 million followers on Twitter, feeds a vast network, not only with her own commercial products but also with views on political issues, such as the reform of health care—a significant item in President Obama's political strategy. Meanwhile new online media, like the American gossip site Gawker, do what celebrity muckrakers have always done. Buzzfeed has built itself a very substantial audience online and an admired business chiefly based upon tabloid content, inventing en route a journalistic genre it calls the 'listicle'—a way of setting out key points in an accessible and inviting manner which has subsequently been copied by newspapers all over the world. In 2013, Buzzfeed announced a $50 million investment in overseas correspondents. Meanwhile, the UK's mid-market *Daily Mail* has achieved the distinction of running the world's most visited newspaper-owned website, where it retails a mix of global celebrity news, drawing on real-time information about reader preferences to position stories on the site. It was fitting that Paul Dacre, editor of the *Daily Mail* since 1992, should have chosen a lecture series in 2007 honouring Hugh Cudlipp, the presiding tabloid genius of the *Daily Mirror*, to remake the argument that commercially successful mass-circulation papers 'need to be sensational, irreverent, gossipy, interested in celebrities and human relationships and, above all, brilliantly entertaining sugar-coated pills if they are to attract huge circulations and devote considerable space to intelligent, thought-provoking journalism, analysis and comment on important issues'.

This is, of course, a self-serving argument, but it is one that the turbulence of digital media has not swept away. We may no longer live in something labelled the tabloid decade, but nor have we left it behind.

Chapter 5
Up to a point, Lord Copper's: who owns journalists?

Journalists are free-spirited individuals: mavericks not easily bound by corporate rule and regulation or, in certain situations, even by the law of their own land. Yet almost all of the Western world's late 20th century journalism, in its heyday of industrialization, took place within the kind of substantial corporate setting which is typically risk aware, subject to regulation, and focused on financial results.

In the 21st century, things may be changing. The Internet, with its diffuse churn of social networks, blogs, and microblogs, has opened or reopened to citizens generally the opportunity to contribute journalism, even if they lack access to a mainstream media outlet. The American journalist A. J. Liebling famously remarked that freedom of the press existed only for those who happen to own one and that is why the Internet has been referred to as 'Liebling's revenge'. This chapter considers the effect on the practice of journalism of shifting forms of ownership and institutional setting.

These days, in spite of a lingering impression to the contrary, most Western news media are not run by press barons. The cigar-chomping tyrant who barks out orders for editorial lines, in between flogging ads and plotting the demise of some nearby president or prime minister, has his roots in the small printing shops of the pre-industrial era, when publishers literally wrote, printed, distributed, and sold advertisements for their newspapers. In the 21st century, big-name media magnates or 'moguls' are rarer than they were 100 years ago, in the days of Pulitzer, Hearst, Northcliffe, and Beaverbrook, when big men (all were male) with big machines rode a wave of industrial expansion and were mostly very explicit about their political views and ambitions. This phenomenon is by no means extinct, but today's mainstream news media movers and shakers in North America and Western Europe are, more typically, focused on mainstream commercial success and, with it, a less brazen form of political influence. They are also, increasingly, infiltrated by corporate and non-corporate players with roots in the digital world, such as Jeff Bezos of Amazon, now owner of the *Washington Post* (see Figure 8), and Pierre Omidyar, founder of eBay and investor in online investigative journalism projects which include *First Look Media*. Meanwhile, digital corporate interests from beyond journalism—Apple, Google, Twitter, and Facebook—are playing

8. In 2013, Jeff Bezos, founder of online retailer Amazon, acquired the *Washington Post*—a symbolic transfer of power to the media barons of the digital age

their own part in reshaping the world of news according to their own priorities.

By the last decades of the 20th century, Britain certainly appeared to be witnessing a second rate wave of media barons: the pornography publisher Richard Desmond, who acquired the *Express*; Robert Maxwell, whose doomed and dishonest self-glorification in the pages of his *Daily Mirror* never seemed anything other than crass, and the Thatcherite Canadian Lord Conrad Black, who gained control of the *Daily Telegraph* and the *Jerusalem Post* and wrote bombastic articles for both, before being thrown in jail for embezzling shareholders' money. Rupert Murdoch, a more serious figure, built a media empire embracing Europe, North America, Australia, and parts of Asia, whilst displaying great skill on both sides of the Atlantic in the synchronized and ruthless deployment of political muscle through teams of journalists who seldom stepped out of line for long. Newcomers, such as the Russian oligarch Alexander Lebedev (owner of the *Independent* and London's *Standard*) have yet to achieve the media stature to support a classic media baron profile.

In the United States, recent years have also continued to witness dynastic succession in parts of the media, with Samuel Irving (Si) Newhouse inheriting and expanding his father's magazine business, which includes high-performing titles like *Vogue* and *Vanity Fair*. Ted Turner inherited only a small billboard company from his father, but he built it into a decent-sized media empire around his 1980 cable news creation CNN. Michael Bloomberg, a Wall Street executive, created a business news enterprise from the success of his data and trading terminals and after 2001 combined this with a long spell as mayor of New York.

In less developed media markets in Eastern Europe, Asia, Africa, and Latin America, the old-style news media baron remains a familiar figure. In the Russia of Boris Yeltsin and Vladimir Putin, 'oligarchs', enriched through privatization of state assets, have proved mostly politically compliant media owners. A version of this pattern can also be observed in several countries of Eastern Europe, such as Romania and Serbia, where matters are complicated by concealment of true business interests by complex holding structures. In India, Subhash Chandra built Zee TV into the strongest broadcaster on the subcontinent and combined this with a range of other media and non-media businesses. Brazil's Roberto Marinho, a businessman with links to his country's military dictatorship, spent 40 years building Globo to be the second-largest television company in the world.

Corporate man cometh

If today's typical American and European news media boss is not a Murdoch or a Ted Turner, what is he or perhaps even she? The most likely answer is a professional business executive, working in a shareholder-owned corporate setting. That corporate setting will most likely entail involvement in a wide range of media, from the Internet to movies, and be spread across more than one geographic market.

The list of the world's top ten media companies (see Figure 9), measured by advertising revenues, according to Zenith Media, is worth a glance. It includes eight US companies and two European, with the probability that, taking into account statistical lags, Baidu, the Chinese search company, should also be in the list. The league table is topped comfortably by Google, with revenues of $38 billion a year, a company which, says its army of critics, has not created a piece of journalism in its life. Nonetheless, its hold on the search gateway to the global Internet (it accounts for over 90 per cent of all searches in Europe) has enabled it to eat into the advertising revenues previously garnered by content companies. The Zenith list shows just how much larger it is than its nearest competitor, DirecTV—a margin of more than $10 billion a

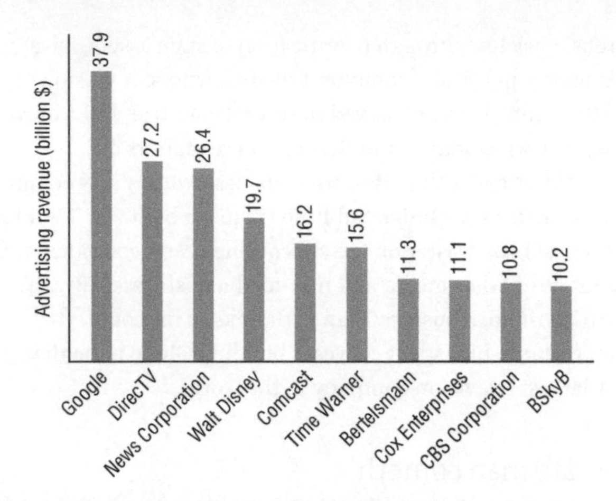

9. Journalists lamented the fact that increasingly they found themselves working for organizations for which news was not the central concern

year in sales. The only company on the list that qualifies as an entrepreneur-dominated entity with a strong history in news is Murdoch's News Corporation, though it too has been cracked apart by adversity in the period since the Zenith compilation. The full list of the top ten also includes Walt Disney, Comcast, Time Warner, Bertelsmann, Cox Enterprises, CBS, and BSkyB. News is not the driver or the principal source of profits for any of these companies. This does not mean that their dominant investors and senior executives lack interest in news or are strangers to the political influence with which it is associated, but it does indicate that the way this influence is used is unlikely to be in the boisterous manner of the classic newspaper mogul.

When press barons ruled the earth

But the hiring, firing, government-toppling press baron remains an important aspect of journalism's identity; a figure often willing to invest in news media when the commercial conditions look least promising.

Most prominent in American legend is Citizen Kane, a figure based on William Randolph Hearst, who in 1898 was said to have precipitated war between Spain and the United States by falsely accusing Spain of blowing up a US battleship in Havana Harbor. Hearst, the story goes, dispatched an artist to illustrate reporters' dispatches, but soon received a cable saying: 'There is no trouble here. There will be no war. I wish to return.' To which the publisher is said to have replied: 'Please remain. You furnish pictures and I'll furnish war.' According to Hearst's son, this legendary reply was in fact never uttered. That it is so well remembered owes everything to Hollywood's *Citizen Kane* where his words are: 'You provide the prose poems and I'll provide the war!'

In Britain, a wholly fictional figure best captures the spirit of the press baron. Evelyn Waugh's comic masterpiece *Scoop* gave us Lord Copper, whose erratic judgement was surpassed only by his stridency. Lord Copper's craven underlings, trying to stay just on the right side of the truth and the boss, developed a standard reply still heard in some newsrooms to this day: 'Up to a point, Lord Copper.'

Most industrialized countries have had their Lord Coppers. In France, the textile manufacturer Jean Prouvost built a press empire which included the daily *Le Figaro*, *Paris-Soir*, and two of the 20th century's most successful magazines, *Marie Claire* for women and the illustrated weekly news magazine *Paris Match*. Since 2004, the Dassault family, best known for its aerospace interests, has owned *Le Figaro*. In Germany, Spain, and Italy, matters were complicated by the rise and fall of fascism. Germany's biggest media group today, Bertelsmann, has its roots in religious book publishing, but the country's dominant newspaper owner, Axel Springer, fits the Citizen Kane bill, even though his firm only began operations in Hamburg in 1946, under licence from the occupying British forces. Springer launched the populist *Bild-Zeitung* in 1952 and by the mid 1960s controlled 40 per cent of the West German press. Like

Hearst, Springer is famed for a single pronouncement—that too much reflection is bad for Germans—and is also immortalized in a work of fiction, Heinrich Böll's *The Lost Honour of Katharina Blum.*

But mostly, the corporate types are overhauling the old-style tycoons. Today, even the American supermarket tabloids, once the personal instrument of owner-publishers like Generoso Pope, are small units in larger publishing groups, enjoying advantages of scale in back-office functions; cross-selling between different advertising markets and wielding greater weight in negotiations for publishing rights to celebrity content and sports rights. It is a matter of heated debate which of these models best serves journalism.

Profits of doom

The case for the press baron is that societies need powerfully led news organizations to stand up to politicians and other wielders of power. A tyrant at the top also reflects the hierarchical structure of the industrial process of the 20th century daily newspaper newsroom: designed for speed of decision taking in a day which starts with nothing but ideas, and ends in the late evening with finished newspaper bundles being thrown into the backs of lorries. The downside is that this structure favours a macho style of management, where bullying can be a useful tool rather than a reportable offence. Authoritarian cultures, in newspapers as in business and politics, are also vulnerable to self-delusion, internal corruption, and cover-up.

The case for the shareholder-owned company is that the business side of journalism is more definitively separated from editorial opinion: the classic separation of 'church' and 'state' which sits at the heart of one idealized model of journalism in democratic societies. The main risk of this arrangement is that the shareholder-owned company is necessarily focused on financial results: in the case of American companies listed on the stock market, this means attention on quarter-to-quarter profits improvement. By incentivizing editors with share options and setting ambitious profits targets in response to Wall Street pressure, newspaper companies like Gannett and Knight Ridder have been accused of distracting editors from journalism's civic purpose and, on the way, damaging reader loyalty vital to the longer-term health of the business.

Leonard Downie and Robert Kaiser, then working for an organization whose formal mission statement declared a willingness to sacrifice profit for service to its readers (the *Washington Post*), took up this theme. Based on interviews with editors, they accused media corporations of demanding from their newsrooms soft features, friendly to local advertisers, and neglecting hard news. They found journalists' jobs and expenses cut, even when advertising was strong, and savagely so during revenue downturns. Gannett, they say, regularly moved editors and publishers around 'so they are relative strangers in the communities they serve'. By 2012, only 38 per cent of American adults considered themselves regular newspaper readers, compared with 81 per cent in 1964. The figures were not much better in the UK, though the newspaper habit was proving somewhat more resilient in Germany and France.

Murdoch, last of the big beasts

How does this picture compare with life on newspapers owned by one of the West's last great dynastic news barons? Rupert Murdoch has certainly invested, sometimes overambitiously, in newspapers and other news media. But he is still pictured on the front of a widely used media studies textbook armed with a knife and fork as he prepares to carve up a vulnerable Planet Earth. Yet, as Colin Seymour-Ure has pointed out, the 35 per cent share of the UK national newspaper market held by Murdoch's News International at the start of the 21st century was smaller than the proportion controlled by Lord Harmsworth a century earlier.

Murdoch, however, has been content to play the bogeyman; perhaps it is the mischief-making journalist in him, along with an astute sense that by presenting himself as an outsider he could ride the wave of political and economic liberalism which gathered in the 1980s and broke in the 1990s. When he arrived in Britain to take over the *News of the World* in 1969, he was asked whether he would interfere in the editorial operation (see Figure 10). He had not, he replied, come from the other side of the world merely to sit back and watch. Murdoch demonology has him firing editors like a bored youth spitting out watermelon seeds and it is true that he has removed talented people who stood in his way, including the respected Harold Evans, who quit the editor's chair at *The Times* live on Britain's main evening television news in 1983. But it is not true to say that Murdoch has routinely operated a revolving door for editors at any of his newspapers. As he explained himself in an interview in 1999: 'If an editor is producing a paper you are basically pleased with and proud of… then he is very safe in his job. If an editor is producing a paper which is clearly failing, turning the community against it,

10. Rupert Murdoch in 1969, after he had acquired the *News of the World*

then you have to make changes. I've been in that position once or twice and been criticised for being ruthless in changing editors, but the people who'll be ruthless are the shareholders, who'll get rid of me if the papers go bust.'

No one much believed Murdoch when, in a speech in London in 1993, he announced that the day of the media mogul was done, but he was at least half right. 'The days when a few newspaper publishers could sit down and agree to keep an entire nation ignorant of a major event are long gone,' he said. 'Technology is racing ahead so rapidly, news and entertainment sources are proliferating at such a rate, that the media mogul has been replaced by a bevy of harassed and sometimes confused media executives, trying to guess at what the public wants.'

In due course, Murdoch would bear witness to the truth of his own words, displaying harassment and confusion in abundance when his *News of the World* was accused, initially in reports carried by the *Guardian* newspaper but later by the police, of allowing or perhaps even encouraging its reporters to hack into mobile phone accounts and other electronic sources in order to get stories. For many months, Murdoch rode this storm, but when it was established that his staff had turned their hacking skills on the phone of the murdered schoolgirl Millie Dowler and her family, Murdoch recognized that he could no longer bluster his way out of trouble. Amid calls for draconian controls on the conduct of journalists, Murdoch closed the *News of the World*, transferred his son James from the top executive position in his UK business, and prepared to be interrogated by committees of MPs and, in 2012, by the judicial inquiry led by Lord Justice Leveson.

'These people are not journalists'

Can we draw any conclusions about which ownership conditions make for a great newspaper or a great TV news channel? Tom

Rosenstiel of the Committee of Concerned Journalists insists that 'the biggest change is that most journalism is no longer produced primarily by companies engaged mostly in journalism'. When Time Inc merged with Warner Communications, about 50 per cent of its revenues came from journalism. With the merger between Time Warner and AOL, journalism accounted for less than 5 per cent of revenues, even though the company still controlled 35 per cent of all the magazine circulation in the United States. 'The values of the people who run that company are very different,' says Rosenstiel. 'These are not journalists in the sense that Henry Luce (*Time*'s founder) was.'

Yet journalism does not always prosper inside news-mad family-owned companies, which can run out of willpower and capital. The Graham family's surrender of the *Washington Post* to Jeff Bezos is an example of a family recognizing its limitations. Has the *Wall Street Journal* done better or worse as a result of its purchase by News Corporation? The *New York Times* remains family-owned and focused on its mission, but this has not preserved it from severe difficulties in the age of digital turbulence, not to mention bouts of troubled journalistic ethics. Some other world-class papers are owned by trusts and other non-profit-seeking collectives (such as the *Guardian* and *Le Monde*); here the big challenge is to combine editorial excellence with sustainable business models.

In the last decade, there have been many experiments in funding new local news services and collectives to sponsor investigative journalism, supported by philanthropic organizations and other sponsors. Web-based 'crowdsourced' funding mechanisms have been used to support journalism projects of many kinds. Changes in commercial business models, involving paywalls, subscription, and micropayments offer new sources of revenue without necessarily implying changes in ownership culture. Meanwhile, non-commercial sources of funding, such as those which support the BBC and other 'public service broadcasters' have sometimes led to decades of excellent and highly trusted news services and sometimes to dull obeisance to a political party line. There is no 'golden rule' to dictate the ideal form of media ownership with regard to good journalism—indeed, experience says that the goal should be to achieve the greatest diversity of institutional forms possible.

Regulation

Commercial markets do not automatically generate healthy competition and diverse approaches to providing service. Competition law, established on more or less agreed principles in most advanced economies, seeks to ensure that no player in any market can acquire and abuse its market power, for example by excluding new competition or fixing prices. The laws in some countries also seek to promote 'plurality' of types of owners of news organizations. Some countries have rules which involve restrictions with regard to the record and character of news media owners. European countries also take the view that 'market failure'—where the commercial market will not deliver news services of a quality and range considered necessary for civic well-being—can be corrected by non-commercial forms of investment, such as public service broadcasting. These issues have caused controversy in most countries at one time or another, exposing severe tensions between commercial news providers and their subsidized competitors.

In recent years, however, with the rise of the Internet, the spotlight of competition authorities in North America and Europe has switched away from companies that provide media content to companies that provide access to that content on the Internet. Google has been the subject of major investigation by competition authorities on both sides of the Atlantic, on the grounds that its dominance of the search market has enabled it to secure a grip on advertising which involves, according to Google's critics, unfair use of the search platform's inside knowledge. During 2012, however, the US anti-trust authorities concluded that the damage being done by Google to media content businesses was more than offset by the scale of the consumer welfare generated by Google's activities. In 2014, the European Commission's investigation into similar issues also failed to deliver the strong anti-Google measures sought by European content companies.

Do journalists care who they work for?

What do the journalists themselves think about these different ownership models? The answer is that they are inclined to grumble a lot, whoever is boss. This goes with the fact that journalists in Western countries have mostly not been good at forming powerful professional associations to regulate their own professional standards or even, in most countries, at running effective trade unions.

Having worked myself for a British shareholder-owned company (Pearson, owner of the *Financial Times*); a publicly owned corporation established by Royal Charter (the BBC); a proprietor-owned magazine (the *New Statesman*), and a newspaper owned by a mixture of British, Irish, Italian, and Spanish shareholders (the *Independent*), I could not say that one 'model' is preferable to another, though it is obviously better as a journalist to work for an institution which is successful, stable, and capable of maintaining a predictable level of investment.

Outstanding journalism was done in all these settings and yet each also had its limitations. At the BBC, journalists see themselves as part of a great tradition of public service and are genuinely committed to standards of accuracy and impartiality, even where definitions of these things involve tortuous introspection. It's also true, however, that the BBC struggles sometimes to keep in check its own bureaucracy, which can militate against the kind of well-judged risk taking on which the most ambitious journalism thrives. Working for the *Financial*

Times, the atmosphere was intellectually bracing, wonderfully international, and committed to getting the facts right. But it could also be too narrowly focused. Every Christmas, we had a competition for the dullest headline of the year and there was never a shortage of entries.

After 15 years at the *FT*, I became editor of the *Independent* during a period when the paper was lurching between shareholders from four countries and where management had been entrusted to executives from the Caligula school of business. They had the power to order waves of budget cuts, to rail against coverage of Africa as an obsession with 'dead black babies', and worse. Somehow, through all of this, writers continued to produce great work, to which readers reacted with a heartening blend of enthusiasm and outrage. We even provided the launch pad for Helen Fielding's *Bridget Jones's Diary*. At the *New Statesman*, a long-established political magazine of the left, we had tight but dependable budgets, so the job involved much coaxing of good writers to contribute to the magazine at a fraction of their normal rates of pay.

Essentially what an editor needs to do the job well is enough money to hire quality journalists, freedom to take editorial decisions, and as much managerial stability as possible. To me the task often seemed to be like that of managing a football club: exciting, turbulent, and hugely rewarding when things are going your way. If you lose the support of the owner, there is no point debating the rights and wrongs. 'It's only a question of when, not if, you get the boot,' Kelvin Mackenzie, the former *Sun* editor, cheerily told me in the back of a taxi one day a few weeks into my tenure at the *Independent*. When a strong editor with good ideas coincides with stable ownership and shrewd business management, there is a chance of magic. But these conditions can arrive, or not, in any system of ownership. Utopian forms of worker control do not achieve much if the advertising department cannot sell space and even the comfortably funded and institutionally well-founded BBC shows every few years that it knows how to lose its way.

Today, the Internet is making possible local news services funded by charitable trusts; individual blogs funded by subscription; crowdsourced investments into new corporate entities and projects; and many other experiments. Journalists, increasingly employed on a part-time or freelance basis, can be forgiven for asking whether the resulting initiatives will be sufficiently well resourced to pay for sustained, inquiring, in-depth journalism, but the diversity itself is surely welcome. Shareholder-owned and proprietor-owned news media are good in the mix, but no longer welcome as a monoculture.

Journalists and their editors are, however, right to be reflective about the business settings in which they work. Adam Michnik, editor-in-chief of *Gazeta Wyborcza*, refused to accept share options in what became an increasingly powerful publishing group in post-Cold War Poland on the grounds that, as editor, he wished to measure himself not by the growth in shareholder value but by the service provided to readers. Agora, the company which owned the newspaper, also set up a charitable trust to hold 7.5 per cent of its stock when it was successfully floated on the stock market in 1999. 'This isn't just a business for us,' said Wanda Rapaczynski, chief executive of Agora. 'Part of being free media, untainted by political interests, is being willing to play a role in the country's democracy. And part of that belief is being committed to broad ownership of this company and giving back to our country.'

At moments of crisis, which all editors experience, editors have to be able to count on their owners. As editor of the *Independent*, I was prosecuted following my decision to publish leaked material from a court case which revealed government duplicity in the overseas sale of armaments. If we lost, the lawyers said, I could go to jail. In the end, we won. Curiously, I never doubted that the *Independent*'s management, with whom I was not on the best of terms, would stand by me at this awkward moment. That, I like to think, says something about the bond between journalists and owners when they face together the test of holding power to account.

Chapter 6
Hacks vs flaks: journalism and public relations

Of the many self-indulging aphorisms beloved of journalists, one of the most comforting states: 'News is something somebody somewhere doesn't want printed. All the rest is advertising.' Sometimes attributed to Lord Northcliffe, the British press baron, it is easy to see why this breezy oversimplification exerts such appeal, portraying the journalist as moral crusader, exposing truth against the odds.

This 'Northcliffe doctrine' does, however, raise a fundamental issue in journalism; namely: in whose interest does the journalist work—for the interest of an employer or for a wider 'public good'? The answer, of course, may be both. To which the follow-up question is: in the event of a clash, which interest takes priority? If journalists in a commercial setting consider their first loyalty is to shareholder interests, it makes it harder for them to draw a sharp line between the value and integrity of their own work and other forms of professional communications or 'commercial speech'.

The more that journalism resembles mere entertainment, or a service brokering paid-for messages into the public domain, the more difficult it is to defend the significant privileges democratic societies afford journalists, such as the qualified right not to reveal sources of information; not to mention the most basic right, subject to laws of libel and contempt, to free expression. The 'Northcliffe doctrine' evades such complexities. According to it, real news simply cannot come from 'official sources' or their PR agents. It must be hard-won. As the journalist Claud Cockburn said: 'Never believe anything until it is officially denied.'

Mau-mau the flak-catchers

Tom Wolfe captured the spirit of the journalist's dismissive view of public relations in his 1970 report on life in San Francisco's anti-poverty programme. Wolfe's portrait of the shifty 'flak-catcher' portrays the official spokesman with nothing at his disposal but hollow words, confronted or 'mau-maued' by an angry group demanding to know why their subsidized job scheme is to be cut back. Wolfe writes:

> This lifer is ready to catch whatever flak you're sending up. It doesn't matter what bureau they put him in. It's all the same. Poverty, Japanese imports, valley fever, tomato-crop parity, partial disability, home loans, second-probate accounting, the Interstate 90 detour change order, lockouts, secondary boycotts, GI alimony, the Pakistani quota, cinch mites, Tularemic Loa loa, veterans' dental benefits, workmen's compensation, suspended excise rebates—whatever you're angry about, it doesn't matter, he's there to catch the flak. He's a lifer.

The uncomfortable fact for journalists today, over 100 years since the birth of the public relations industry, is that there are in the United States many more flak-catchers (or 'flaks' as reporters sometimes call them) than journalists (or 'hacks', as journalists sometimes call themselves). And where the USA leads, others follow. Nor do today's flak-catchers merely or mainly seek to block the hacks' flak: rather they seek to pre-empt it, deploying numerous and ingenious tools and stratagems to get the journalists to see matters their way.

The justified fear among journalists is that they are losing this battle because of disparity in resources. Public relations people, especially those working in the upper reaches of financial, corporate, and government public relations, are better paid than all but a handful of very senior or celebrity journalists; they also tend to have steadier jobs, sometimes with better access to technology and other resources. 'The trouble with journalism today,' one senior PR executive told me, 'is that the journalists we deal with tend to be rather young, not very experienced and stretched by the number of deadlines they're running against. You often feel that you are dealing with people who really don't understand the story. That's quite scary.'

Journalists, however, are less than honest if they say that they do not make use of public relations contacts and other official sources of information. Some may want to swagger, with Claud Cockburn, but in reality journalists use any relevant source of information they can tap. A journalist covering a beat naturally wants scoops and ready access to top people: the decision takers and primary sources. But this is not always realistic: top people are, by definition, busy, so they surround themselves with intermediaries, whose specialism it is to deal with the 24/7 world of news. Skilled reporters recognize that there is a hierarchy of sources for information and that you don't go to your best contacts for routine facts, or to check history.

Journalism and 'churnalism'

But lazy journalists, or those without the necessary time and skills, can and do become overdependent upon intermediaries, reproducing uncritically whatever ready-made material comes their way. As long ago as the 1950s, Scott Cutlip showed that nearly half of what filled the pages of American newspapers came from public relations channels. In 2006, Nick Davies, an investigative journalist from the *Guardian*, commissioned Cardiff University researchers to establish the origin of information in five of the UK's leading newspapers over a random two-week period. They analysed 2,207 domestic articles and concluded that 60 per cent of the material 'consisted wholly or primarily of wire copy and/or PR material, and a further 20 per cent contained clear elements of wire copy and/or PR to which more or less other material had been added'. The researchers concluded: 'These data portray a picture of journalism in which any meaningful independent journalistic activity by the press is the exception rather than the rule.' Davies took these findings as clear evidence of what he called the spread of 'churnalism' across a landscape of 'Flat Earth News', where unreliable or partisan information is recycled as 'news'.

This conclusion may be too harsh—not least because it assumes that all this 'gifted' source material is unreliable. Today's public relations practitioners say that knowingly putting out misleading information generates unacceptably high levels of risk because of the likelihood, in a world rich in social media, that distortions or errors will be embarrassingly exposed by consumers or activists. At the same time, it is true that social media enable news providers to make use of video, photographic, and other material supplied by members of the public, whose own affiliations are mostly obscure. The most careful news organizations attach a 'health warning' to such contributions, but many do not. Sometimes news organizations deliberately disguise the provenance of media content, as with the 'advertorials' they routinely publish in magazines and newspapers with the financial support of specific advertisers or sponsors, or the online version of this practice: so-called 'demand media'. These activities provide grounds for caution against the loftiest claims of the hacks with regard to the role of flaks. A little history also helps us to understand just how deeply entangled these two worlds are.

How journalists created the PR industry

The first recognizable public relations agency was born in Boston in 1900, but the word 'propaganda' has its origin in the

17th century Roman Catholic Church's 'Congregatio de Propaganda Fide'—propagating the faith. Public relations emerged as part of modern industrial management in the early 1900s when the USA engaged in one of its periodic backlashes against excessive business power. Soon, every self-respecting business had a team of lawyers to deal with the competition authorities and professional communicators to promote its cause with journalists and the public. The obvious place to recruit these communicators was from newspapers.

William Wolff Smith was a reporter for the *Baltimore Sun* when he opened his 'publicity business' in Washington in 1902 and he continued to operate as a 'stringer' or part-time correspondent for a number of newspapers, while supplying pieces reflecting the interests of his clients. Rockefeller's first public relations 'counsellor' was Ivy Ledbetter Lee, son of a Methodist preacher from Georgia, and a former police reporter on Hearst's *New York Journal*. Lee joined the Rockefeller payroll in 1914, following his skilful work in handling the aftermath of the company's bloody assault against striking Colorado mineworkers and their families (the 'Ludlow Massacre'). One of the radical journalists who reported the massacre, George Creel, went on to make his own name chairing the Committee on Public Information, which propagandized within and on behalf of the United States during the First World War. After the Armistice, Creel's vast programme released into the American private sector a demobbed army of PR experts, who built the modern public relations industry. Edward Bernays, a sometime reporter and Broadway theatrical press agent, also worked for the Creel committee, before starting his own PR agency in 1919.

Engineering consent

Lee was clear that, for his techniques to succeed, his clients must show integrity in order to win trust. Only honest companies would meet 'the high demands of enlightened public sentiment'. Others took their calling even more seriously. Walter Lippmann's seminal book *Public Opinion* recommended the application of social scientific techniques to measure and shape public attitudes. Meanwhile Bernays, nephew of the psychologist Sigmund Freud, set out a classic text:

> The [PR] counsel directs and supervises the activities of his clients wherever they impinge upon the daily life of the public. He interprets the client to the public and he interprets the public to the client. Perhaps the chief contribution of the public relations counsel to the public and to his client is his ability to understand and analyse obscure tendencies of the public mind. He first analyses his client's problem—he then analyses the public mind.

It was a short step from Bernays's pioneering thoughts to his concept of 'engineering consent' for the client organization's goals. To some, this sounded too much like hypnosis and propaganda of a menacing kind. They argued that the public relations practitioner had 'an ethical duty above that of his clients to the larger society'. Bernays took the view that effective and factually accurate arguments from business and other organizations were a necessary element in a well-functioning democracy. We can see public relations, barely out of its infancy, caught in a moral dialogue closely resembling the one still taking place today about journalism.

These grandiose notions have, however, encountered very many predictable difficulties, as one PR firm or another has snatched the cash rather than pausing to make any sort of ethical reflection. Ivy Lee's own career ended in shame when it turned out he was a paid adviser to I. G. Farben, the German chemical giant which assisted in Hitler's attempted extermination of the Jews.

Not quite on the same scale, but probably more morally devious, were Hill and Knowlton's actions in the war which followed the invasion of Kuwait by Iraq in 1990. Employed by the Kuwaiti monarchy at a fee of $12 million to promote its interests inside the

United States, the firm established a front organization called Citizens for a Free Kuwait. This, in turn, proceeded to manufacture stories about Iraqi atrocities in Kuwait. Nayriah, a sobbing 15-year-old girl, testified to a public hearing of Congress's Human Rights Caucus on 10 October 1990. She reported that she had seen Iraqi soldiers taking babies out of hospital incubators and leaving them 'to die on the cold floor'. Shortly afterwards, she was identified as the daughter of the Kuwaiti ambassador. Hill and Knowlton also spent years conveying the tobacco industry's case that its products were not to blame for lung cancer. Out of such hard-bitten experience John Hill, one of the firm's founders, advanced a less morally high-flown definition of the goals of public relations as 'the management function which gives the same organized and careful attention to the asset of good will as is given to any other major asset of the business'.

Spin doctors in the thick of it

But it was in the sphere of politics that public relations became most controversial. Hamilton Wright, whose early career included a spell on the *Los Angeles Times*, built the first public relations organization devoted to promoting the interests of overseas countries. One of his techniques was to make a contractual guarantee to his clients that the money they paid him would buy at least five times as much publicity as the equivalent amount spent on advertising. Much later, in 1964, the Public Relations Society of America censured the firm, by then run by Wright's grandson, for violating a rule which forbade pledging 'the achievement of specified results beyond a member's direct control'. But the accused man simply quit the society and carried on business as usual, illustrating another similarity between public relations and newspaper journalism: its resistance to any form of truly independent regulation.

More momentous was the work in 1930s California of two ex-reporters, the husband-and-wife team of Clem Whitaker and

Leone Baxter, who came together to fight and win a local referendum. Flushed with this success, they formed Campaigns Inc, the first professional campaign consultants, a breed which has dominated every American election campaign since. In Whitaker's own words, they transformed campaign management from being 'a hit or miss business, directed by broken-down politicians' to being 'a mature, well-managed business founded on sound public relations principles, and using every technique of modern advertising'.

The vigour of their legacy is today evident all over the world; from the rise of Bill Clinton to the presidency of the United States to the community-building social media campaigns of Barack Obama; from the modernization of the British Labour Party under Tony Blair, which in turn influenced Gerhard Schröder's leadership of the German Social Democratic Party (SPD), to the strategy of Lionel Jospin's Socialist Party in the late 1990s. Philip Gould, a senior communications adviser to Blair, wrote extensively about the lessons 'New Labour' learnt from Clinton's New Democrats: 'a highly disciplined set of communications techniques, most of them learnt from business public relations and marketing, including sophisticated data management to track voter opinions, identify possible switchers and ensure instant rebuttal of hostile points'.

Any journalist exposed to these methods can testify to their zeal. A few weeks before the UK's May 1997 general election, I was editing the *New Statesman*, a political magazine which had developed a reputation for springing unwelcome stories. One day, just before dispatching the final pages to the printer, I took a telephone call from the Labour Party's headquarters, to be told: 'I'm calling from the Rapid Rebuttal unit. Could you tell me what you are putting in the magazine this week, so that I can prepare a rebuttal?' One overenthusiastic spin doctor in Tony Blair's government was forced to resign when it was revealed that she had sent an email on the day of the terrorist attacks on New York and Washington in September 2001, pointing out that this would be a good day 'to bury some bad news' about local government expenditure.

Gould always denied that there was anything exceptional or morally questionable about spin, which he defended as 'a longstanding and completely unexceptional activity. In a world in which political parties, and other high-profile organizations, are under twenty-four hour media attack, it is common sense to employ people to put the view of the party or the organization and to do it to best effect. In a modern media environment, competence and good communications are inseparable: you cannot have one without the other.'

Gould is certainly right that Ivy Lee and John Hill were spin doctors before Tony Blair was born. But these early public relations figures were operating in a world where the news media were less powerful and certainly less ubiquitous than at the turn of the 20th century. Piers Morgan, who edited the *Daily Mirror* during part of the Blair premiership, has revealed that in a period of about nine years, he lunched or dined with the prime minister on no fewer than 18 occasions and met him a further 30 times for private chats or interviews. It emerged during the Leveson inquiry into newspaper ethics in 2012 that Rupert Murdoch and/or his senior executives had met the then British prime minister David Cameron on no fewer than 59 occasions between 2006 and 2011.

For anyone focused on policy, the combined effect of spin and aggressive shifts in journalistic culture was debilitating. In the words of Geoff Mulgan, who spent seven years at the helm of Blair's policy strategy group, the gap between public perception and reality has become so large that it 'promotes the idea that there are no truths, only strategies and claims'. By the time of his second landslide victory in 2001, Blair was busily attempting to dispel the idea that his was a government of 'spin, not substance'. Once out of office, he openly attacked the 'feral beasts' of the news media and, in his memoirs, expressed bitter regret for a much welcomed and important Freedom of Information Act, which he said had simply handed more power to reporters and made the work of government more difficult. An unhappy epitaph.

Money makes the spin go round

When it comes to the business world, the patterns of spin are even fiercer, camouflaged as they are by the operation of high-speed global markets. The US media analyst Howard Kurtz wrote (in 2000) that 'the world of Wall Street spin is...a daily, dizzying match in which stock prices, corporate earnings, and millions of individual investments are riding on the outcome...In this overheated environment, the degree to which basic facts can be massaged, manipulated, and hyped is truly troubling. And that raises the fundamental question: amid the endless noise, whom do you trust?'

The overlapping interests of market traders, investment analysts, corporations, shareholders, and journalists present vivid temptations, including to journalists. In the dot-com boom of the late 1990s, journalists from the *Daily Mirror* in London and the *San Jose Mercury News* in the United States were caught lining their pockets using information gathered in the course of their journalistic activities. Many expected the then editor of the *Daily Mirror*, Piers Morgan, who had traded stock on the basis of his city desk's inside tips, to be fired, but he retained the support of the company, until eventually a bigger, ethical scandal involving faked pictures forced him from office.

Richard Lambert, editor of the *Financial Times* throughout the 1990s, acknowledged the failures of business journalists to spot the dubious business practices that came to light in the 2001 crash of the Houston-based energy company Enron. 'The signs of Enron's impending difficulties were there for anyone who cared to look,' he says. So why did business journalists fail to spot them? 'Because they were too influenced by the views of big financial institutions, many of which rated Enron a "buy" to the bitter end; because too much business journalism today is concerned with personalities rather than hard analysis and because business, unlike politics, is largely conducted without transparency and behind the protection of fierce libel laws, especially in Britain. One of the main tasks of the media is to hold power to account. With no serious alternative to free market capitalism, governments are increasingly obliged to enter into relationships with corporations. An intelligent examination of business starts to become a crucial component of democratic choice.' Lambert's words remind me of a much older and simpler story from the earliest days of the *Financial Times*, when its young chairman, Horatio Bottomley, found himself stitching mailbags in jail, following his involvement in a mining industry scam. A visitor sighed: 'Ah, Bottomley, sewing?' to which the disgraced publisher replied: 'No, reaping.'

Trust bust

The digital world is changing public relations as much as it has changed journalism. Now threats to reputation can emerge out of a clear blue sky not just from a small-enough-to-be-manageable corps of journalists, but from an isolated blog or video that goes 'viral' or through a Twitter storm. Professional communications experts have responded to the challenges involved, acquiring new skills from 'search engine optimization', designed to ensure that internet searches lead to positive rather than negative information on their clients, to the darker technique of sweetening clients' Wikipedia entries and stirring up their own carefully instigated Twitter campaigns, a device known as 'astroturfing' to indicate its goal of artificially manufacturing positive expressions of grass-roots opinion. Social media techniques to build online communities for businesses such as retailers have much in common with the nurturing of networks of fans in music and sports, as well as in politics, where the 2012 re-election campaign of President Barack Obama was much admired.

What is at stake is reputation—in what PR firms call 'the reputation economy'. Surveys over many years indicate that politicians and journalists languish at the bottom of most league tables of public trust, whilst recent surveys (such as the Edelman

Trust Barometer of 2013) point to a growing gap between trust in institutions, including businesses and public sector organizations, and trust in the people who lead those businesses. Only one in five people told Edelman that they trusted business or governmental leaders to tell the truth. In Philip Gould's account of spin, he recalls advice from David Hill, considered a more 'old school' communicator in the Labour Party ranks, that: 'You have to never tell a lie—telling lies is disastrous, because one of the most effective elements in being a spin doctor is that they believe what you are saying to them.' This loss of reputation for leaders has corrosive effects across society.

I had my own experiences on the PR side of the communications fence between 2003 and 2010, when I worked first as director of corporate affairs at BAA plc, a company which at the time owned most of the UK's airports. I then worked at the Foreign and Commonwealth Office as director of strategic communications

At BAA, we managed the company's stance with regard to the controversial environmental issues arising from growth in demand for flying. Then, in 2006, the company was the subject of a successful takeover bid. My own approach to communication in both these aspects was to insist upon open engagement with the media and other stakeholders based upon rigorously accurate information and transparently evidenced judgements.

When, in 2008, I went to work for David Miliband, the UK foreign secretary, my mission was to help this geographically sprawling and rather conservative part of government embrace the opportunities of digital media. Guided by our belief in what Joseph Nye has called 'soft power', we worked with partners on numerous campaigns, from the London Olympics to political change in Burma. Soon we had 'digital diplomats' vying with each other to demonstrate their social media community-building skills in their own areas of expertise. These proved highly effective.

An ephemeral but ironic crowning glory occurred at the Group of 20 Summit in London in 2009, where our global online campaign prepared the ground for Prime Minister Gordon Brown to coordinate early responses to the 2008 banking crisis. The event went well and even momentarily perked up the prime minister's poll ratings, but within 48 hours of his triumph, Brown was surrounded by scandal, provoked by the work of one of his aides, Damian McBride, an out-of-control 'dark arts' practitioner inside Number 10 Downing Street. From here, Brown never looked back as he slithered to defeat at the 2010 General Election.

In his book *Dark Art*, ex-journalist and PR man Tim Burt argues that traditional PR techniques of media management are no longer effective in a world of resource-depleted mainstream journalism and uncontrollable social media. Burt's conclusion, which in my view is correct, is that the PR industry has no alternative but to encourage its clients to be truthful: 'Today's media environment demands public relations without spin.' He is, however, surely too optimistic in stating that 'the practice of "dark arts" may be coming to an end'.

There is no sign yet that the erosion of trust that has spread such a cynical rot through politics and business is close to a turning point. Deterioration in standards of professional behaviour by some journalists, public relations people, politicians, and business has contributed to this state of affairs. In 2009, I was invited by Taylor Bennett, a UK firm specializing in the recruitment of PR executives, to make a pithy contribution to a compendium of points of advice from an array of London-based PR chiefs. Perhaps I put it a little too bluntly by writing that 'if what you're saying isn't sufficiently authentic and truthful to be worthy of trust, then you have a moral obligation to keep your mouth shut'.

Chapter 7
Murder is my meat: the ethics of journalism

Journalism is a domain of high-velocity moral choices and tense emotional situations, which probably explains why the news media have proved such a fertile source of cinematic storylines.

These celluloid heroes have come in many shapes and sizes, reflecting the concerns of their day. In the 1930s, Torchy Blane, a female reporter, tested gender stereotypes in the urban jungle, demanding entry to crime scenes with the words: 'Holdups and murders are my meat. I'm Torchy Blane of the Star.' Orson Welles's *Citizen Kane* (1941), based upon the career of William Randolph Hearst, explored his subject's inability to distinguish between fact and fiction. 'He was disappointed in the world, so he built one of his own,' says one of Kane's aides. Billy Wilder's *Ace in the Hole* (1951) flopped at the box office but earned classic status with its story of an unscrupulous reporter who ruthlessly manipulates a mine rescue drama. There have been no fewer than four screen adaptations of *The Front Page* (1931), a play which includes Hildy Johnson's uncomfortably accurate description of the general news reporter's life: 'It's peeking through keyholes. It's running after fire engines, waking up people in the middle of the night. It's stealing pictures off little old ladies after their daughters get attacked.' In *Five Star Final* (1931), Edward G. Robinson's rag delights in ruining the lives of essentially blameless people. Confronted by the daughter of a woman who has killed herself rather than face further humiliation by headline, Robinson snatches for the newsman's standard defence. 'Newspapers', he says, 'are only great mirrors that reflect the world.'

In the 1970s, Hollywood's mirror briefly reflected a more positive image of newsroom life. *All the President's Men* (1976), starring Robert Redford and Dustin Hoffman, told the story of the decade:

11. Journalism's moral mission can be high-minded—no more so than in the exposure of the Watergate scandal by reporters from the *Washington Post*, rendered iconic in a subsequent Hollywood movie

the *Washington Post*'s exposure of the Watergate conspiracy (see Figure 11). These scenes made glass-walled offices de rigueur in newsrooms around the world. Soon Jane Fonda was exposing nuclear skulduggery in *The China Syndrome* (1979), and Clark Kent, *Daily Planet* reporter turned Superman, made his own transition from comic book to cinema screen. But the sunnier mood didn't last. Films like *Broadcast News* (1987) showed journalistic integrity taking second place to glamour and entertainment, and *The Insider* (1998) portrayed television journalism corrupted by corporate self-interest. The first edition of this book referred to a study which identified more than 1,000 American examples of journalism as the subject of films. Since then, Brian McNair has combed through UK cinema releases from 1997 to 2008, logging a further 72 titles. No clear thematic pattern emerges, but his log indicates the vitality of the genre: from an admiring account of David Frost's 1997 on-air skewering of President Nixon (*Frost/Nixon*, 2008) to *Shattered Glass* (2003), which finds 'new media' turning over 'old media', in this case the magazine *New Republic*. McNair commends *Rag Trade* (2005), panned by most critics, but admired here for 'the sharpness and effectiveness with which it explores British tabloid news culture… a style of journalism from which all ethical and moral foundation has been removed'. More recently still, *The Fifth Estate* (2013) explored the moral dilemmas of the WikiLeaks affair.

Journalism kills

If Hollywood's journalists are ethically challenged, so too in real life. On 15 October 1978, Rupert Murdoch's *News of the World* published a story about a maths teacher, Arnold Lewis, who organized sex parties for consenting adults in his caravan in the Welsh hills. When an undercover reporter phoned Lewis to tell him that the story would soon be splashed across the paper, Lewis gassed himself. At the inquest, the female reporter whose byline appeared on the story was asked by the coroner whether the contents of the dead man's suicide note upset her. 'No, not really,' she replied. Many years later, her editor confessed that the incident still kept him awake at night.

Do journalists take ethics seriously? It varies. One of the most widely used textbooks in the training of British journalists comments that to put 'journalism' and 'ethics' in the same sentence 'is to risk reducing the listener to helpless laughter'. Graham Johnson, a self-styled 'tabloid terrorist' reporter for the *News of the World* and the *Sunday Mirror*, among others, told all in a book, *Hack*. Rich in examples, the book sums up by saying that Johnson and his colleagues 'lied for a living, cheated members of the public and broke the law routinely'. Or, as Kelvin Mackenzie, celebrated editor of the *Sun* during the 1980s, once put it: 'Ethics is a place to the east of London where the men wear white socks.'

Piety at the *Post*

There is an aspiration to greater piety elsewhere. The *Washington Post Desk Book on Style* reiterates the principles laid down when Eugene Meyer bought the paper in 1933. It begins: 'The first mission of a newspaper is to tell the truth as nearly as the truth may be ascertained.' Among its other solemn pronouncements is this: 'The newspaper's duty is to its readers and to the public at large, and not to the private interests of the owner. In the pursuit of truth, the newspaper shall be prepared to make sacrifices of its material fortunes, if such course be necessary for the public good. The newspaper shall not be the ally of any special interest, but shall be fair and free and wholesome in its outlook on public affairs and public men.'

The *Post*'s manual runs to more than 200 pages. Yet, according to one study, the verbosity of such news organization 'bibles' conceals some glaring omissions. Of 33 American newspaper manuals analysed by the Poynter Institute in 1999, fewer than one in five codes addressed the subject of editorial and advertising department tensions and many codes ignored the crucial subject of how newspapers do or do not actually enforce their standards, as opposed to proclaiming them.

The public interest exception

In Britain, the BBC's guidelines for producers are also book-length, taking in rules on everything from impartiality (required by law in the case of all licensed UK broadcasters), fairness, privacy, taste and decency, violence, the depiction of children on television, conflicts of interest, and much else. The *Editor's Code of Practice*, upon which the British Press Complaints Commission based its adjudication of complaints against newspapers, is a four-page document that gives a good indication of the central ethical standards which journalists in many parts of the world regard as ethically relevant. These are:

- Accuracy, and the prompt correction of inaccuracies.
- The opportunity to reply to attack or criticism.
- Prohibition of invasion of privacy, including by long-lens cameras, except in cases involving genuine public interest.
- Harassment is forbidden, except in cases of public interest.
- Intrusion upon people suffering grief or shock must be 'made with sympathy and discretion'.
- Children should not be bothered at school or, under the age of 16, interviewed or photographed without parental consent.
- No use of listening devices, or phone tapping, except in cases of public interest.
- Hospitals: journalists should not operate covertly.
- Misrepresentation: 'Journalists must not generally seek to obtain information or pictures through misrepresentation or subterfuge.' Such information 'should be removed only with the consent of the owner'. Again, there is a public interest exception.
- An individual's race, gender, religion, sexual orientation, or disability is only to be mentioned in stories where directly relevant.

- Financial journalism: no use for personal profit of information received; no writing about shares in which a journalist has an interest, without permission of the editor.
- Confidentiality of sources must be protected. This is 'a moral obligation'.
- Payment for stories is acceptable, but not where payment is made to criminals or their associates. Again, there is a public interest test.

The self-regulatory approach of the UK Press Complaints Commission (PCC) is important, not least because it is based on a very long tradition of press freedom and as such has been emulated in recent years within emerging democracies in the Balkans, Asia, Africa, and elsewhere. The PCC also played a key role in developing a global network of self-regulatory press bodies around the Alliance of Independent Press Councils of Europe. These initiatives are not to be confused with the World Association of Press Councils, a body accused of providing a front for state-dominated media organizations, intent upon a censorious global code of ethics for journalists reminiscent of the 'world information order' promoted in the 1980s by UNESCO.

The case against the PCC has always been that its rhetoric is strong but its powers are weak, and that it is anything but independent. Funded and, essentially, governed by newspaper publishers and editors, its only sanction is to oblige newspapers to publish its adjudications. Its activities never prevented newspapers, on a daily basis, violating almost every item in the code. Because so many of its rules may be broken on grounds of 'public interest' (defined as anything which exposes crime, protects public safety, or prevents the public being misled), even those rules which appear strong are, in practice, negotiable. Celebrities can, it is routinely reasoned, justifiably be exposed because a story about a private sexual misdemeanour is at odds with the star's 'image'. Convicts and police officers can be bribed because it helps unmask wrongdoing. These days, it is also routine for newspapers to pay for information (a practice once known disapprovingly as 'chequebook journalism'), with the result that many stories arise from financial motivation, commonly when a professional sex worker is paid to divulge his or her account of time spent with a circulation-boosting celebrity.

The American way

In the United States, there is no PCC. Individual newspapers or newspaper groups deal with complaints directly and many have 'readers' editors' or ombudsmen with specific powers to consider complaints and seek correction, right of reply, or other form of adjudication.

American journalism, however, also faces serious ethical challenges. According to a survey of nearly 300 journalists in 2000, self-censorship was commonplace, much of it resulting from journalists bending to pressure from financial sponsors or advertisers—a problem especially acute in local media. More than a third said that 'news which would hurt the financial interests of a news organization goes unreported'. A previous survey, in 1999, showed that journalists increasingly felt their work to be less accurate, that 'the lines have blurred between commentary and reporting', and that 'pressure to make a profit is hurting the quality of coverage'. Half of the journalists questioned thought that their credibility with the public was a major issue. It was to combat this perceived decline in public respect that the Committee of Concerned Journalists came together in 1997, launching its Project for Excellence in Journalism. The project has uncovered data which suggested that only 21 per cent of Americans think the press cares about people, down from 41 per cent 14 years earlier, and that less than half thought the press valuable in protecting democracy. Thirty-eight per cent believed news organizations to be actually 'immoral'.

But the same research also discovered that American journalists are surprisingly united in their core values, especially in their belief that journalism's central purpose is to hold power to account and to provide the resources of information and opinion upon which democracy thrives. 'News professionals at every level... express an adamant allegiance to a set of core standards that are striking in their commonality and in their linkage to the public information mission,' concludes one piece of research. On the other hand, the project also confirmed a growing sense of conflict between the goals of the businesses which own the news media and these civic principles. So, although 'every mission statement on file with the American Society of Newspaper Editors names advancing self-government as the primary goal of the news organization', corporate lawyers 'advised news companies against codifying their principles in writing for fear that they would be used against them in court'.

Truth, loyalty, and verification

Bill Kovach and Tom Rosenstiel, leading figures in the American movement to uphold traditional standards of journalism, worked up from this research a set of nine principles which are more general in character than the codifications of the PCC, or broadcaster guidelines, but which seek to identify the characteristics they believe the news media must adopt if they are to be trusted and fulfil their democratic mission. Here is the list:

- Journalism's first obligation is to the truth.
- Its first loyalty is to citizens.
- Its essence is a discipline of verification.
- Its practitioners must maintain independence from those they cover.
- It must serve as an independent monitor of power.
- It must provide a forum for public criticism and compromise.
- It must strive to make the significant interesting and relevant.

- It must keep the news comprehensive and proportional.
- Its practitioners must be allowed to exercise their personal conscience.

New news isn't so sure

This is a good list but it is also, as any first-year media studies student schooled in the subtleties of situational ethics and moral relativism will tell you, rather old-fashioned. Kovach and Rosenstiel acknowledge that 'the truth' is no longer, if it ever was, uncontested. In 1992, Jon Katz, the journalist and cultural critic, proclaimed in the pages of *Rolling Stone*: '[S]omething dramatic is evolving, a new culture of information, a hybrid New News—dazzling, adolescent, irresponsible, fearless, frightening and powerful. The New News is a heady concoction, part Hollywood film and TV movie, part pop music and pop art, mixed with popular culture and celebrity magazines, tabloid telecasts, cable and home video.'

To this, Kovach and Rosenstiel responded: 'We understand truth as a goal—at best elusive—and still embrace it.' This unalterable goal is, they say, endangered by the 'new' journalism: its speed, the anything goes spirit of the Internet, and the need for journalism to exaggerate in order to stand out from a bigger and more jostling crowd. This is 'creating a new journalism of assertion, which is overwhelming the old journalism of verification'. Traditional skills supporting verification, they might have added, such as shorthand and the law, are simultaneously being neglected.

To the outsider, the vigour of this debate, which peaked in the 1990s, looked like a promising self-defence against complacency in journalism, especially as it was supported by the resources of the Pew Centre for the People and the Press, which makes possible quality data for research as a basis for serious debate. In Britain, there was a low rumble of assent to some of these ideas, accompanied by big talk. 'Print journalism is now the most corrupt realm of life in Britain,' wrote one national newspaper journalist in 2002. 'Some journalists boast of lifestyles that are little more than perpetual junkets—bribes—from those whose news they report.' Or to cite an earlier clarion call, at the launch of the *British Journalism Review* in 1989: 'The business is now subject to a contagious outbreak of squalid, banal, lazy and cowardly journalism whose only qualification is that it helps to make newspaper publishers (and some journalists) rich.'

A philosopher calls

In recent years, there has been a growing debate outside the journalism profession about these matters. In her Reith lectures of 2002, the philosopher Onora O'Neill took the theme of trust and directed her argument at a press guilty of 'smears, sneers and jeers, names, shames and blames... If the media mislead, or if readers cannot assess their reporting, the wells of public discourse and public life are poisoned.'

The ethic of truthfulness, or more modestly accuracy, does indeed lie at the heart of journalism. Without it, journalism devalues its own civic currency by undermining trust. Industry codes and the law of the land have a part to play in setting the necessary standards, but as we have seen in the financial services industry, which is regulated in minute detail, this does not necessarily eliminate serious wrongdoing. That is why Kovach and Rosenstiel are right to insist upon truth telling and, in their ninth and final article of faith, to turn to the conscience of the individual journalist.

Working with young, would-be journalists in a journalism school, you encounter real and justified nervousness about the newsrooms that lie ahead. Is it all right to apply emotional pressure to a parent who has lost a child in tragic circumstances to hand over a treasured picture? Is it OK, as Hildy Johnson suggests, to steal the photo from the mantelpiece? What about stealing a document, or a glance at a document when your interviewee is momentarily distracted or called from the room? In what circumstances would you lie to get a bigger truth? Would you ever be prepared to disguise or conceal your identity? It depends, doesn't it? It would be acceptable to pose as the purchaser of a dodgy car in order to expose a dealer whose business is in selling dodgy cars. But to pose as a doctor, in order to get someone to tell you a celebrity's health secrets? Could such intrusion be justified on the 'public interest' grounds that the subject of the inquiry is famous? What about if the goal was to expose dangerously lax standards at the hospital? In these sorts of cases, codes only get you so far and, in any case, what is forbidden in one news organization may be regarded as a matter for celebration in another. How else to make sense of a professional world which extends from the *Washington Post*'s rule that 'in gathering news, reporters will not misrepresent their identity' to custom and practice on the late *News of the World*, whose most famous reporter habitually dressed up as a sheikh in order to entrap victims? When journalism students ask how they should navigate through a world of such contrasts, it is difficult to make any other reply than this. Journalists are part of the societies in which they work. They acquire, within those societies, a sense of right and wrong; they have a moral compass learnt outside journalism. It is up to every individual to preserve that compass, to be true to their own and their civic community's values. In a healthy workplace, the culture of the news organization will also guide you well. But you can't always trust your news editor. You must know how to say no.

Who are these journalists anyway?

If we are to depend, as we must, on journalists and their consciences, supported by healthy newsroom cultures, quality training, and wise guidelines, we also need to know more about journalists, to reassure ourselves that they are broadly representative of the rest of us. So who are they, these journalists, and to what extent do they share values?

These questions are not so easily answered as may be imagined since there is no very clear agreement on how to define a journalist. Does the definition include, say, news presenters, who may be actors rather than people trained in news? Does it include radio talk show and tabloid TV hosts; does it include someone who sets up a blog and shares information and opinion with anyone willing to pay attention? What about researchers on a television documentary, or researchers on an entertaining quiz based on the news?

In Britain, the number of journalists is subject to a wide range of estimates. Some put the figure as low as 15,000, others as high as 120,000, though the best guess is probably in the 60,000 to 70,000 range. A rare piece of research in 2002 gave us a snapshot of the essential characteristics of contemporary British journalists:

- As likely to be a woman as a man.
- Young: 70 per cent of journalists are under 40.
- Childless: only 23 per cent have dependent children.
- White: only 4 per cent are from ethnic minority groups.
- Metropolitan: 55 per cent work in London and the South East.
- Middle class: only 3 per cent of new entrants have parents who are unskilled or semi-skilled.
- Graduates (98 per cent).
- Low paid: the average salary was £22,500, though stars earn more than ten times that level.

This survey was repeated by the National Council for the Training of Journalists, with minor changes, at the end of 2012 at the culmination of the Leveson inquiry discussed below. Given the turbulence of the intervening decade, it was perhaps surprising that so much had remained the same: newspapers were still the main employers of journalists; it was still primarily a middle-class, gender-balanced, ethnically un-diverse, and metropolitan occupation.

But behind these continuities lurk some significant indicators of change: pay had fallen by 12 per cent in real terms; 28 per cent of journalists were now self-employed and many indicated that they work in a range of media for a range of employers. Many combine journalism with non-journalistic forms of employment. This new hybridity in the organization and status of journalists presents a significant threat to any narrow or highly disciplined definition of a professional culture of journalism. A quarter of British journalists also reported that their work sometimes involved pressure on ethical boundaries and only 29 per cent said they had confidence in the regulatory apparatus (of 2012) which applied to journalism. Most sadly of all, asked whether they would recommend journalism as a career to a young person, only 51 per cent said they would.

The global journalist

Professor David Weaver of Indiana University has worked for many years with a group of academics around the world, attempting to throw light on facts about journalists on an international basis. His most recent collation of data (with Lars Willnat), published in 2012, took in surveys involving 29,000 journalists scattered across 31 countries over a five-year period. Given this diversity, Weaver hesitates to identify commonalities, but he does conclude that 'the typical journalist is still primarily a fairly young college-educated man who studied something other than journalism in college, and who comes from the established and dominant cultural groups in his country'. He adds, however, that women are catching up on men in journalism and that 'the average proportion of racial and ethnic minorities also has risen'. In terms of the 'watchdog' role of journalism, the authors report a confused picture. On ethics: 'The only practice that seems almost universally agreed upon is not revealing news sources who have been promised confidentiality. There are large differences of opinion on whether it might be justifiable to pay for information, to pose as someone else, to badger or harass news sources, and to use a personal document without permission.' They conclude: 'What seems certain is that a culture of global journalism has not yet emerged.' One response to this vacuum, proposed by media scholar Peter Berglez, is a concept of 'global journalism', designed to encourage the effective reporting and analysis of the many themes which require coverage beyond any set of national borders: subjects such as climate change, the economy, and migration.

Lord Footnote?

In 2012, British newspaper journalism was convulsed by a scandal of unprecedented proportions. A judicial inquiry, led by Lord Justice Brian Leveson, was set up by Prime Minister David Cameron in July 2011, following revelations about the misbehaviour of journalists on Rupert Murdoch's *News of the World*. The immediate detonator of controversy was the news, first reported by the *Guardian*, that the paper's reporters had in 2002 hacked the mobile phone of a murdered schoolgirl, Milly Dowler. This information emerged from a long chain of events about *News of the World* wrongdoing, including the criminal prosecution in 2007 of Clive Goodman, the paper's royal editor, for which he was jailed. Through all of these years of what Rupert Murdoch would later call 'a cover-up', the *Guardian* went on digging and the Press Complaints Commission reprimanded the *Guardian* for its actions. Within days of the prime minister's announcement, Murdoch closed the 168-year-old *News of the World* (see Figure 12).

Lord Leveson's terms of reference were to examine the culture, practices, and ethics of the press, though this was later broadened to include consideration of electronic news media. There were to be three areas of focus: the press and the public; the press and the police; and the press and politicians.

By the time of his initial report in November 2012, Leveson and his counsel had interrogated 337 witnesses and received statements

NEWS OF THE WORLD

July 10, 2011 Edition number 8,674 £1

The world's greatest newspaper 1843-2011

THANK YOU & GOODBYE

After 168 years, we finally say a sad but very proud farewell to our 7.5m loyal readers

INSIDE: 48-PAGE SOUVENIR PULLOUT

PROFITS FROM THIS HISTORIC EDITION WILL GO TO CHARITY

NAMED SHAMED

CAUGHT!

FERGIE 'SELLS' ANDY FOR £500k

HUNTLEY IN HIS CELL

FREE INSIDE

JACKO'S DEATHBED

12. The phone-hacking scandal in Britain forced Rupert Murdoch to close the *News of the World*, the title upon which he had built his British newspaper business

from a further 300 individuals or organizations. The witnesses included A-list celebrities, more humble victims, front-rank politicians, editors, and publishers. His almost 2,000-page report began by noting that this was the seventh big inquiry into UK press standards in less than 70 years. When I appeared to give my own evidence, Leveson himself interrupted the interrogation by his counsel to make points that were clearly right at the front of his mind: he had no interest in constraining press freedom; he was not in any sense 'anti-tabloid'; and he was determined not to be 'another footnote' in the kind of book people like me write.

In his report, he cited Thomas Jefferson that 'where the press is free and every man able to read, all is safe'. But, he said, the press also had responsibilities 'to respect the truth, to obey the law and to uphold the rights and liberties of individuals'. The PCC, he said, was not fit for purpose, showing no capacity to constrain newspapers which, when the story was hot, showed no respect for the codes of practice editors had themselves devised. As a result, offending newspapers had 'wreaked havoc with the lives of innocent people'. He detected 'a recklessness in prioritizing sensational stories'. He proposed 'a genuinely independent and effective system of self-regulation'. In order to ensure that this happened and that the new body performed to the required specification, there would be legislation to ensure the independence and effectiveness of the new regulator, to enable the new regulatory system to benefit from new legal incentives to encourage better behaviour, and to enshrine in British law for the first time the principle of a free press.

Prime Minister Cameron, it quickly became clear, was not comfortable. Although the big newspaper publishers probably did not welcome an open fight, they had made it clear that they would not tolerate legislation, citing a centuries-deep tradition of a press unregulated by Parliamentary statute. Initially, Ed Miliband, the Labour Party leader, came out for full implementation of Leveson's proposals. Then a counterproposal to legislation emerged, in the form of a Royal Charter (the BBC is established by Royal Charter). It looked like the press might be playing for time, as it had done in previous battles, confident that the closer it got to the next general election (due in 2015), the less robust the politicians would become. At the time of writing, it looks like the national newspapers will again seek to make their own rules and regulations without reference to the new Royal Charter, and so perhaps consign Lord Leveson, as he feared, to the footnotes of media history. Meanwhile, the UK's courts continued to handle 100 or so criminal cases connected to illegal hacking and other crimes, including bribing public officials and perverting the course of justice. Among the defendants was Andy Coulson, former editor of the *News of the World* and the prime minister's former communications director.

My own views on the Leveson debate were set out in my evidence to the inquiry. I advocated a form of statutory underpinning for a genuinely independent self-regulatory body. I also argued (as did Leveson himself) that Ofcom, the UK's communications regulator of which I was a founding non-executive director, was now a sufficiently experienced body to act as the 'verifying agent' for this independent regulator. Was all of this, as the newspaper publishers said, an outrageous assault on press freedom? Not in my view. Perhaps by the time you read this, a workable and healthy compromise will have at last emerged. I hope so; but I doubt it.

Chapter 8
Digital: after the deluge

For a couple of years at the end of the 1990s, as the dot-com boom peaked, the world of journalism went crazy. It was impossible to be among journalists without hearing of someone who was leaving their job to set up a web-based news service, blog, or e-zine or to work for someone in California. There were so many jobs, it became difficult to recruit into journalism training courses. Who needed training when there were jobs galore for anyone with enthusiasm and a bit of dot-com attitude?

It was also a time when everyone pushed to be in everyone else's business. Newspapers could see that the Internet would steal readers and classified advertising, but what was the best way to fight back? Some created specialist websites for advertisers to keep them loyal; others rented space and set up online offshoots. Magazines rushed to establish new brand identities online and in television. Television piled into interactive services. Mergers seeking to add value from this 'digital convergence' were the toast of the stock market.

Some gambled billions. Others merely doubled the size of their editorial staffs. 'What the hell were we all smoking that weekend?' was the question asked a few years later at Time Warner, according to Rupert Murdoch, reflecting upon the decision by the American media giant to sell itself into a merger with America

Online at the very peak of dot-com valuations. Never in the history of journalism has a new wave of media emerged so rapidly and with such volatile consequences.

Dot-com bust

What happened next was, for journalists, much less amusing. The dot-com bust, as media revaluations reconnected with reality, did not mean that the digital communications revolution had been stopped in its tracks. It signalled the start of the most painful decade for professional journalism in over a century, at least for those working in news organizations in the 'mature' media markets of Europe and North America. As news publishers struggled to adopt new ways of working, it became clear that the Internet was anything but an easy diversification option for established players. Rather, it was inaugurating a new, global information ecology, in which there were brand new players, with skills and insights the news industry lacked and, in some cases, short-sightedly scorned. Among those threatening the status of professional journalists were, in Jay Rosen's words: 'the people formerly known as the audience'. 'User-generated content' became a routine input to journalism, whether in the form of front-line witness or the more deliberate activity of bloggers, now able via social networks to reach worldwide audiences as easily as any professional news organization. The news industry's barriers to entry had been blown off their hinges.

New beasts on the block

Soon the new beasts on the block were roaring: especially the Internet 'platforms' through which the news media would, from this point, need to work. Google (born 1998) emerged as the decade's dominant search company, able to 'aggregate' news and so become, as many customers saw it, their main supplier of news, even though the company employs no journalists. Facebook (born 2004) turned an idea born of a wheeze in a college dorm into a global social network, racking up over a billion subscribers as the zone of the news ecology closest to personal and domestic life. A 2013 Pew Research study found that 64 per cent of American adults used Facebook and that of these almost half were picking up news there.

Then came Twitter (born 2006), a microblogging service where messages are limited to 140 characters, and which had 500 million users by 2012. Twitter quickly found roles relevant to news: as a signalling tool for professional journalists driving traffic to their own web platforms, and as a quick and cheap way to post pictures, video, and text from news scenes via mobile phones, which by 2010 provided a core and affordable global network. Twitter was important in some of the period's biggest stories: the 2010–11 political ferment known as the Arab Spring and the riots which swept across London in 2011. In this same dramatic decade, with traditional news publishers on the down escalator and Internet platform companies riding in the opposite direction, Apple (born 1976) reinvented itself as a new type of electronics company, with its multimedia iPhone (2007) and then its iPad and 'app' store, where people could buy software enabling them to read newspapers and magazines on-screen, in comfort, offline: establishing yet another point of intermediation where cash which had once gone to news publishers was diverted to Silicon Valley.

The decade of doom

These and countless other 'new media' services flourished most extensively at first in the world's most prosperous countries, but soon made an impact everywhere. They transformed the way that people gathered, edited, accessed, and consumed news, with consequences that are by no means exhausted at the time of writing. The new online or 'born-digital' players quickly offered advertisers cheaper and more effective ways of reaching audiences, because the new information ecology also yielded rich 'Big Data' about user habits and preferences. This had very severe consequences for newspapers, which until then had relied more on advertising than on cover price. Who needs to buy a newspaper to check out jobs or apartments to rent if all the data you need are freely available and easily searched on a computer or mobile device?

By the end of the first decade of the 21st century, the picture in terms of lost revenues, closed or curtailed titles, and lost journalists' jobs in North America and Europe was grim. Between 2000 and 2012, the number of people employed in American newsrooms fell by 30 per cent from over 56,000 to below 40,000 as sales of daily newspapers tumbled from almost 60 million to 44 million (see Figure 13). Newspaperdeathwatch.com recorded that a dozen metropolitan dailies went under between 2007 and 2012. *Newsweek* magazine, first published in 1933, abandoned print in 2012, following its merger with the born-digital *Daily Beast*. London-based *Lloyd's List*, the world's oldest newspaper, followed suit. The authoritative Pew Research Center 'State of the News Media' report in 2013 found shrinking newsrooms in cable television and increased use of robotic editing techniques in 'a news industry that is more undermanned and unprepared to uncover stories, dig deep into emerging ones or to question information put into its hands'. Pew warned that in the wake of newsroom cost-cutting, almost one in three respondents to a public opinion survey said they had deserted a news outlet because 'it no longer provides the news and information they had grown accustomed to'.

In the UK, the news industry's pain intensified in the second half of the 'decade of doom', when the structural problems caused by the Internet were aggravated by the economic downturn which followed the collapse of Lehman Brothers bank in 2008. By 2013, the UK's biggest-selling daily newspaper, Rupert Murdoch's *Sun*, had sales of 2.4 million, down by a third from its level in 2000. The *Daily Mirror*'s sales in the same period had more than halved to 1.1 million, falling far behind the middle-market *Daily Mail*,

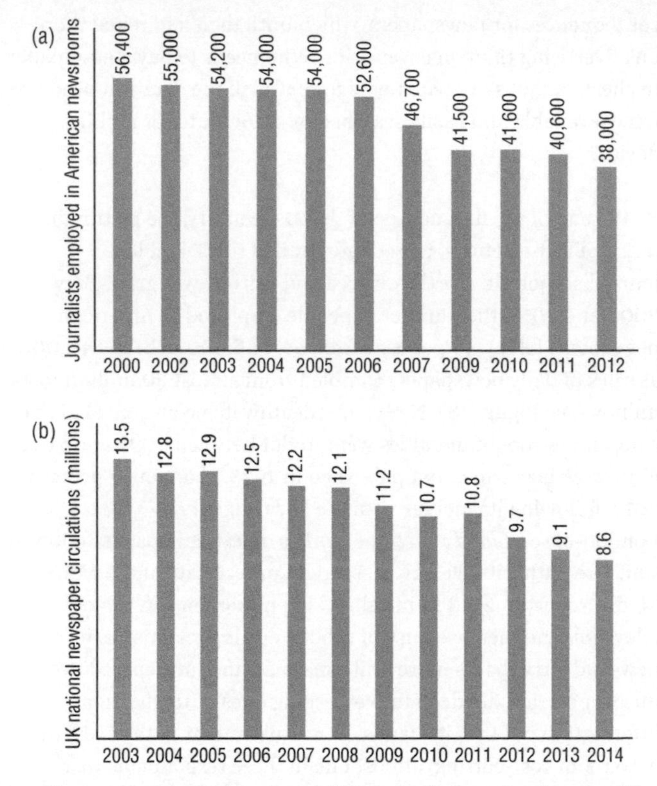

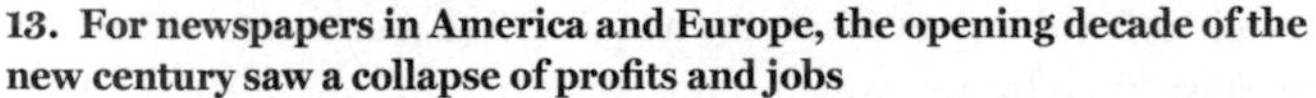

13. For newspapers in America and Europe, the opening decade of the new century saw a collapse of profits and jobs

whose sales fell 'only' by half a million to 1.9 million. *Press Gazette* reported that between 2005 and 2011, 242 local newspapers had closed and 70 new titles launched. Sales of *The Times* had fallen by half to below 400,000.

In Western Europe as a whole, the sales decline in the five years to 2012 was roughly 12 per cent; countries with less centralized newspaper industries (i.e. more regional newspapers) held up better than very centralized countries like the UK. Germany saw a wave of newspaper distress which sent publishers scurrying to the country's federal government to demand stronger copyright laws to prevent aggregators like Google siphoning off their advertising revenues. *Bild-Zeitung* retained its position as Europe's biggest-selling newspaper, but with sales of 3.2 million daily—compared with over 5 million in the 1980s. French publishers successfully asked their own government to lean on Google to provide €60 million to fund French digital media initiatives.

These impacts on journalism and the news industry have reshaped public debate. In the United States, we moved, in the space of five or so years, from commentators grumbling about the perils of 'infotainment' to lamentations foreseeing the death of journalism.

The fifth estate

Yet as things went from bad to worse, there was an alternative perspective on this cataclysmic interpretation of events. For a start, it was clear that broadcast news was more resilient to the challenges of online competition, especially where investment in public service television made it less dependent upon advertising revenues. Television companies were enjoying thick new seams of revenue through subscription models and catch-up and replay technologies which provided new ways to build audience and extract commercial returns. In the UK, the BBC enjoyed all these advantages, including receipt of a 'licence fee' worth over £3.6 billion a year, and was able to create a market-leading online news service, whilst also successfully defending its audience for television news. In the UK in 2013, television was still a regular source of news for 78 per cent of people, compared with just 40 per cent for newspapers. Newspapers, aggrieved at this taxpayer-funded competition from its outset nearly a hundred years earlier, had every reason to step up their anti-BBC editorial hostility, but from the general public's point of view, the stability of broadcast news services alleviated public concern about the diminishing reach of newspapers.

At the same time, Internet enthusiasts became increasingly confident that something new and substantial was emerging in the space previously dominated by the advertising-funded, professional news industry. This new information system would not provide so many journalists with comfortably salaried positions, nor necessarily be in such a good position to deliver important and valued types of journalism, such as in-depth investigative reporting or sustained reporting of local courts and councils. It would, however, offer access to a great diversity of new talent, energy, and ideas. From the reader's point of view, the Internet made it possible to cruise for news and background information and analysis not only in sites devoted to news, but across the entire worldwide web, where it was now easy to find information provided by academics, scientists, think tanks, non-governmental organizations, activists, and many other sources.

This new information ecology, often likened to the collaborative mechanics made possible by open software standards, has been given many names, among them the 'networked fourth estate', the 'fifth estate', the 'conversational commons', the 'information ecosphere', the 'networked public sphere', and 'open journalism'. Its cheery spirit is well captured in the title of a book by the American writer Clay Shirky: *Here Comes Everybody*. The idea of a 'fifth estate' explicitly challenges the authority of the 'fourth estate'—a political label attached to the English press in the late 18th century, recognizing its importance as an emerging constitutional force, in competition with the more ancient 'estates' of parliament, church, and crown.

The argument from the fifth estate was that journalism of the 20th century, organized around weighty institutions, depended too heavily upon an advertising-funded commercial model and expensive production and distribution systems. Barriers to entry were high, putting plurality of viewpoint at risk from concentrations of ownership, and giving press barons too much power. Some also argued that professional journalism had taken advantage of these arrangements to erect impregnable defences around its own culture, resisting challenge to the news industry's disinclination to acknowledge error or to penalize bad behaviour by journalists.

The Internet appeared to offer relief from these constraints. Just as Wikipedia, the continually updated, multilingual, and vast online encyclopedia had destroyed the monolithic *Encyclopedia Britannica*, so would new publishing platforms and social media offer new ways of gathering, verifying, and distributing news, using the collaborative networks of the Internet. Together with a smaller 'professional' news industry, this would ensure that the classic mission of journalism could not only be sustained, it could be enhanced. The fifth estate would inform people reliably, promote debate, and hold power to account.

When, at the end of this troubled first decade of the century, American journalists and newspaper publishers lobbied Congress for subsidies, using the argument that in the early days of the Republic, postal subsidies for newspapers had been a critical source of support for an industry crucial to the growth of democratic practice, they found that some members of the fifth estate were not on their side, accusing news publishers of special pleading on behalf of an industry in trouble because of its own slowness to innovate.

Drudge reports

An early stand-out figure in online journalism was Matt Drudge (see Figure 14), who entered into public consciousness as a Hollywood-based, one-man-band doing star gossip and movie ratings. Suddenly, in January 1998 he had the American news media at his feet, when he learned that *Newsweek* magazine, owned by the Washington Post group, had held back from publishing an account of President Clinton's sexual liaison with a White House intern, Monica Lewinsky. Drudge, who had been following the rumours about Clinton for some time, got confirmation of the story from a New York literary agent, wrote his report, and dispatched it to his readers. Although it is likely that this story would have surfaced without Drudge, the scoop became a point of definition in American journalism, the e-Watergate of its day, precipitating a scramble for follow-ups.

Here, in Drudge's own breathless words, is what he said it felt like at the point of dispatching that momentous Drudge Report of 9.02 pm, Pacific Time, 17 January 1998:

> Nothing left to do.
> My finger's poised over the button.
> This is everything.
> Everything you've ever been and everything you'll ever be...
> *'Whaddya think yer doin', Drudge?...'*
> Cat. Bummer.
> *'Am I reading this right? You're about to accuse POTUS* [the President of the United States] *of having it off with an intern? Are you preparing to blow up Washington? Get me Janet Reno...!'*
> 'Hey, I don't like it either, but it's confirmed confirmed confirmed, and your Janet Reno's authorized Starr to move in...'
> *'You are a terrorist, aren't you?'*
> Mommy and Daddy were liberals...
> *'You and your internet manifesto.'*
> Let the future begin.
> *'So be it...'*
> Microsoft mouse moved into position.
> Ready. Aim. ENTER.
> Bouncing beams from dish to dish, e's, faxes & alarms. 1 am.
> Cellphones, conference calls, dirty dresses, cigars. 2 am.
> Subpoenas. Grand Juries. Fallout. 3 am.
> Elections. Impeachment. 4 am.
> Acquittal. 5 am.
> Fame. 6 am.
> Dawn.

14. Blogger Matt Drudge was one of the first to emerge from 'the din of small voices' by reporting scandal in the White House

Note the penultimate line. Fame. Drudge, the outsider, was playing for media celebrity. Six months later, he was a guest of the National Press Club in Washington. During his remarks, he spoke of 'an era vibrating with the din of small voices'. He went on: 'Every citizen can be a reporter, can take on the powers that be. The difference between the Internet, television and radio, magazines, newspapers is the two-way communication. The Net gives as much voice to a 13-year-old computer geek like me as to a CEO or Speaker of the House. We all become equal.'

Drudge in his early years wore a trilby hat, in homage to 1920s muckraking journalists, and his early supporters saw him carrying a torch for the journalistic tradition of Tom Paine. The reaction at the Press Club, however, was not so favourable. Doug Harbrecht, the *Business Week* journalist then serving as Press Club president, led the inquisition, and Drudge scratched hard into his shaky knowledge of American journalism to defend himself. But his return fire took casualties. The high-speed, rolling, error-prone editions of online journalism he likened to the heyday of the yellow press, when newspapers would turn out a dozen editions a day. If he made mistakes, he said, so did the august news organizations represented in the room. Then he added: 'I put my name on every single thing I write. No "Periscope" here. No "Washington Whispers" there.' Moreover, he said, he was committed to 'cover media people the way they cover politicians... How did a story like Monica Lewinsky break out of a Hollywood apartment? What does that say about the Washington press corps?' The media, he said, 'is comparable to government— probably passes government in raw power', so had to be interrogated. As for the rules of journalism, concerning the number of sources needed to establish a reliable fact before publication, Drudge said: 'I follow my conscience... conscience is going to be the only thing between us and the communication in the future, now. And I'm very happy with my conscience.'

Harbrecht asked whether Drudge foresaw 'a separation of media practices where future journalists accept more your style and methods, or accept the methods of *appropriate* journalism'. Note the menace in that word 'appropriate'. The only problem Drudge could see was that, if there were thousands of reporters like him clamouring for attention, 'it could start looking like an insane asylum'. But if that happened, 'I think people will grow disinterested. But again, they'll rally around something else. So I leave this to the free marketplace.' Where, Harbrecht persisted, did this leave the 'professional ethic of journalism'? To which Drudge replied: 'Professional. You see, the thing is you are throwing these words at me that I can't defend, because I am not a professional journalist. I am not paid by anyone.'

In the first edition of this book, I speculated that ten years later, Matt Drudge might have vanished without a trace, or that he may be fronting the most popular talk show on network television.

Actually, he is still blogging (<http://www.drudgereport.com>), but he is also a regular on Rupert Murdoch's Fox network and so more firmly labelled in his political loyalties.

All the news that's fit to click

At the start of the 21st century, there was still room for debate about the scale of the challenge facing journalism and its institutions from digital communications technologies. Traditional or 'legacy' journalism, as it was sometimes bleakly called, could still point to the quality of the work of professional journalists in familiar, stable media formats, in contrast with what was characterized as the rumour-mongering chaos of the web. Newspaper publishers felt that they would have time to adjust to new technologies; so they commenced a rather leisurely paced series of experiments. Some secured their online content behind 'paywalls' and charged subscribers for access. These quickly realized the downside: smaller levels of readership and so an intensified struggle to keep advertisers happy. Others preferred an 'open' model online, but then struggled to achieve digital advertising rates comparable to those available in pre-Internet times. There was also a halfway house, where limited quantities of news were free, but heavy users had to pay.

The problem with advertising on the Internet was that there was much more competition than in the oligopolistic markets of print's heyday, so digital ad rates were low. For years, newspaper publishers and their shareholders watched with dismay as profits slumped, with no sign of recovery. If any comfort could be found, it was that many other 'content businesses' suffered similar disruption from the Internet: the music industry and book publishers prominent among them.

By the second decade of the 21st century, it was clear to everyone—journalists, investors, and the public—that newspapers, some magazines, and even parts of the television news industry would have to adapt or die. Even news providers which maintained big audiences, such as the main evening news bulletin on the most popular television channels, faced the challenge of a disappearing younger audience, now apparently content to assemble fragments from the social media networks at the centre of their way of life.

Paul Dacre, a highly successful editor of the UK middle-market newspaper the *Daily Mail* from 1992, told a meeting of his staff as late as 1999 that he had heard a lot of people saying the Internet would be the future for newspapers, adding, to murmurs of satisfaction from the assembled throng: 'I say to that: bullshit.com.' Six years later, Dacre launched the Mail Online, claiming in 2008 that 'our tardiness avoided us losing the millions that others expended', indicating a reverse truth about the digital economy—it may destroy your own barriers to entry, but it has not yet erected barriers in the opposite direction. By 2013, Mail Online (<http://www.mailonline.com>), which does not charge for entry, was the most visited newspaper-owned website in the world, with 138 million monthly visitors, having perfected the art of algorithmically programmed celebrity sleuthing for a younger version of the newspaper's print audience.

All newspapers and most magazines have gone through their own version of the turbulence experienced by the *Daily Mail*. There is no reliable template for success. By 2010, a number of newspapers in Europe and North America were reporting a smaller gap between the decline in their analogue print revenues and the growth in their digital revenues. The *Financial Times*, for which I worked for 15 years, pursued a paywall strategy online, calculating that its specialist content, of interest in business centres around the world, would continue to be 'must purchase' not only for existing print subscribers but also potentially for new readers in centres unreachable by a printed newspaper. Even so, the *FT* had to negotiate a tricky transition from a print environment, in which its price per page or column inch to advertisers was stable and well understood, to a predominantly digital environment, where unit prices were both lower and unstable. By 2014, the *FT* was well into positive territory with 629,000 paying customers, more than half of them online—the highest circulation figure in the paper's history.

Another UK newspaper, the *Guardian*, pursued an entirely different course. A left-leaning paper, it began life in 1821 as the *Manchester Guardian*. Today, it is owned by the Scott Trust, a charitable body whose primary mission is to sustain the newspaper, with the aid of income from its other assets, which include commercial media. One of the *Guardian*'s most distinctive traits is the long tenure of its editors, of whom there have been only ten since 1821. Alan Rusbridger, the current editor, has been in post for almost 20 years and so (like Paul Dacre of the *Mail*) has seen the digital communications revolution from its inception.

As many broadsheet newspapers moved to a tabloid format in the 1990s, the *Guardian* chose the more distinctive (but larger and more expensive to print) *Berliner* format, before locking into an increasingly determined open-access 'digital first' strategy, which has led to extraordinary growth in its readership and influence outside the UK, especially in the United States. As its print circulation dipped well below 200,000, the *Guardian*'s online readership surged to 84 million unique visitors per month in 2013—for an estimated total readership in excess of 90 million, most of it outside the UK. Its annual financial losses, however, also soared, breaking the £40 million barrier in 2012, before declining towards the stated goal of a 'sustainable level of loss'.

Rusbridger calls this approach 'open journalism'—encouraging the maximum ease of access for readers, but also for collaborators in creating content. On a number of occasions, the *Guardian* has appealed to its readers to help sift vast data files. The paper has also collaborated internationally with partners like WikiLeaks (discussed below), the *New York Times*, and *Pro Publica*, a US foundation which supports investigative journalism. These American collaborations not only provide a larger pool of resource, they also enable the *Guardian* to locate particular operations within US legal jurisdication, where the paper enjoys protection from the First Amendment. Rusbridger's critics say that with a staff in excess of 700, he has not done a good job of controlling his editorial cost base, thereby putting the paper's future at risk. Viewed from any other perspective, however, the *Guardian*'s ascent to global influence and status—the third most-read online newspaper in the world, behind the *Mail* and the *New York Times*—makes for a pretty extraordinary achievement. Rusbridger has said that he can imagine the end of the printed *Guardian* within five to ten years.

The *New York Times*, founded 30 years after the *Guardian*, is owned by the Sulzberger family and also has a hugely popular web presence, which works behind a partial paywall. Its business strategy, subject to fits and starts, did not prevent a fall in revenues in every year between 2005 and 2013, as growth in digital revenues failed to offset a bigger decline in print/analogue income. Newspapers everywhere found that advertising sales teams, used to selling column inches, were not well equipped for a world of digital marketing, which demanded complex data analytics about customer preferences and attention to building new communities of interest. The sale of the company's interests in Boston, the appointment of a chief executive from the UK television industry, and the renaming of the *New York Herald Tribune* as the *International New York Times* were all part of the attempt to improve this situation—to make a powerful brand punch its weight in the global digital marketplace.

As newspapers everywhere tried to navigate this print–digital switchback, other players in the news business, such as magazines, radio, and television faced a less intense version of the challenge. Some magazines, such as the UK's long-established satirical fortnightly *Private Eye*, remained defiantly and exclusively available in its own version of newsprint and retained a healthy circulation. The *Economist* successfully exploited a balanced print, online, and app offer, and the *New Yorker* continued to deliver high-class, long-form magazine journalism across platforms. The *New Statesman*, which I edited in the late 1990s, built an online operation of sufficient scale to boost revenues, along with 'brand extensions', such as events. The *Independent*, now owned by a Russian oligarch, launched a very low-priced 'quality tabloid' which found an audience but struggled financially. London's evening newspaper, the *Standard*, previously a paid-for daily with a slithering sale, switched to a giveaway to commuters and, boosted by more advertising, reversed its decline. City *Metro* titles pursued the same approach in several countries.

By 2014, with the economies of Europe and North America growing again, it was possible to think that the worst of the digital storm might have passed. Newspaper business models had adjusted and new types of digital journalism were also well established. These included 'data journalism', which brought together technology experts and journalists to mine, analyse, and visualize 'stories' from the 'Big Data' harvestable from the Internet. 'Live blogging', a format which established itself first in sports reporting, enabled reporters to cover live events through direct observation, whilst also 'curating' access to a wide range of links offering additional perspectives and media. This offered a neat way for a newspaper with, say, a right- or left-wing political stance to draw in contending opinions. Meanwhile, news organizations redesigned their physical and virtual newsrooms, to make them better equipped to collaborate with readers and other contributors, making extensive use of social media networks. The *Guardian*'s coverage of a wave of urban riots which spread through UK cities in the summer of 2011 provided a striking example of the way that reporters were able to combine traditional eyewitness reporting with curation of text and other online feeds to establish a more informed version of the unfolding story. In a follow-up, the newspaper then worked with university academics to provide a reflective assessment of events, based upon analysing a wide range of data sources.

The Internet also provided a peerless, global research tool, supported by rapid if not yet perfect translation of languages; it enables journalists to work in text, audio, or video; and through Twitter's 'trending' index and other web analytics, it offers in real time a sense of the level of interest in a story or theme. At their most sophisticated, computer alogrithms can even be deployed to identify what is likely to be of most interest to readers. This 'robotic' approach to news selection comes with a serious attendant risk—the so-called 'filter bubble', which traps users inside the limited horizons of their previous choices.

Digital natives versus digital adaptors

As news organizations around the world have struggled to adapt to the digital world, they have also had to deal with competition from entirely new players in the news market. Some of these, like Google and Facebook, are involved in news as a by-product. Others have entered the news fray as digital natives, believing that they can identify amid the bloodbath of a newspaper industry fighting for survival wholly new business and editorial opportunities, using new techniques of engagement to attract audiences for news, especially among younger audiences.

The most widespread phenomenon of this kind has been the blogging movement, which emerged (as 'web logging') in the early 1990s via open software, available to anyone wishing to establish a real-time, online personal platform, for use as a public diary or pulpit to the world. Andrew Sullivan, a well-known British journalist, and a former editor of the American magazine *New Republic*, identified blogging in the first years of the new century as 'the first journalistic model that harnesses rather than merely exploits the true democratic nature of the web'. Sullivan proclaimed:

> [A] writer no longer needs a wealthy proprietor to get his message across to readers. He no longer needs an editor, either. It means a vast amount of drivel will find its way to the web. But it also means that a writer is finally free of the centuries-old need to suck up to various entities to get an audience. The universe of permissible opinions will expand. It's no accident that a good plurality of American bloggers are libertarian or right of centre. With a couple of exceptions the established newspaper market in America is dominated by left-liberal editors and reporters. What the web has done is allow talented writers to bypass this coterie and write directly to an audience. If the Drudge Report pioneered the first revolution of this kind, then bloggers are the vanguard of the second wave.

Sullivan's blog, launched in 2000, is still going strong, though today it sits behind a paywall (<http://www.dish.andrewsullivan.com>).

The Huffington Post started in 2005 as an ambitious news aggregator and blog. Like the Drudge Report, it was named after one of its founders, Arianna Huffington, who became the site's editor-in-chief after its sale for $315 million to AOL in 2011. Available in a range of languages and with 'local editions' in major American cities, the Huffpo is advertising-funded and blended instantly into the mainstream of American journalism. Huffington's contributors include well-established journalists, as well as experts from many fields. The blog has even won a Pulitzer Prize.

If the Huffington Post is the website that might have emerged from an established publishing house, Buzzfeed is its cheeky young cousin. Started as a 'viral lab' in New York in 2006 by Jonah Peretti, also a co-founder of the Huffington Post, it has become a highly successful social news and entertainment website, with its trademark formats of lists, quizzes, jokes, and videos: 'the kind of things you'd want to pass along to your friends'. By early 2014, it was boasting 60 million monthly unique visitors and financial break-even, after absorbing $46 million of investment. Buzzfeed, unlike newspapers and the fixed television news bulletin, was built for an age in which the fiercest competition for the audience's time came from Facebook and its multitude of rivals, such as the picture-blogging site Tumblr and the ultra-ephemeral Snapchat.

Buzzfeed's content has more in common with the playful end of the tabloid newspaper than other types of news, but its techniques have been widely copied. One daily newspaper editor told me that Buzzfeed-style lists in his own paper were showing up as consistently the most read and most liked items, in everything from sports to business and politics: the ten worst decisions made by this government; the five best goals of the weekend, and so on. This was around the time that Buzzfeed announced a major investment of $50 million in hiring experienced journalists, specializing in areas such as investigations and data analytics, taking the organization's staff to more than 300 people, many based outside the USA. It should also be added that in this same period Buzzfeed was accused of carrying stories that turned out to be hoaxes, fantasies, or just plain jokes—a characteristic throughout the history of tabloid journalism.

Early in 2014, Peretti circulated a public memo to his own staff, reflecting upon his own recent reading of David Halberstam's 1979 book, *The Powers that Be*, which discussed the emergence of an earlier generation of American media companies. What struck Peretti was the charge against *Time Magazine* that it was guilty of taking stories already carried in newspapers and making them easier to read and more engaging for a new audience. Here was confirmation of the Buzzfeed mission. He wrote: 'It feels like we're at the start of another formative era of media history where iconic companies will emerge and thrive for many decades... Buzzfeed has a real shot to be one of the great, enduring companies of this new era.'

One of Buzzfeed's younger competitors is Upworthy, a viral video-based news site which styles itself as a purveyor of 'things that matter' and urges its users to 'pass 'em on'. Launched in 2012, it took Upworthy only two years to get to a roughly similar reach as Buzzfeed achieved in eight. Its founder, Eli Parisier, the man who coined the term 'filter bubble' (in a 2001 book) to warn of the paradoxical risk of isolation for the social media user, told a South West by South West (SXSW) audience in 2014 that 'there's no purity in doing the beautiful thing that doesn't reach anyone'. This born-digital version of the tabloid editor's taste for headlines of mass appeal ties in with Upworthy's approach, distinctive in its use of capital letters. Picked on the day I happened to be writing this section, the site leads with a video headlined: 'He Used To Recruit For Them. Now He's Working Against Their Messsage. And They Want Him Dead.' The subheading reads: 'Here's what moral courage looks like.' Would you be inclined to click through? I know I would and did. Parisier's background is in Internet activism rather than journalism, having played key roles in MoveOn.org, an important campaigner on left-of-centre issues and for the election of Barack Obama; and Avaaz.org, a more internationally focused campaigner on human rights and other issues. In his SXSW appearance, Parisier defined his editorial goals as 'importance, satisfaction and quality' and said that the Upworthy community's priority issues were climate change, income inequality, and human rights.

Whether Buzzfeed or Upworthy or born-digital competitors like Gawker or Vice.com will last for decades, like the *New York Times* or the BBC, is impossible to say. It seems more likely that in an atmosphere of permanent revolution on the Internet, both the rise and fall of media players will be faster than in times past. We can be sure, however, that the Huffington Post will not be the last online newcomer to be purchased by a big 'legacy' media group. We are, indeed, in a formative era of media history.

Local and hyperlocal

Away from the struggle between national and international news organizations, another digital battle is being played out within smaller communities of interest and communities of place.

For communities of interest, served in the pre-digital era by specialist newsletters and other physical media, the Internet has been a one-way street to more abundant provision. Specialist media, such as newsletters and magazines aimed at professional groups such as dentists, social workers, petroleum engineers, or IP lawyers, have never experienced difficulty charging for their products, so the lower costs of digital distribution flow readily to the bottom line. Illicit copying remains an issue for such businesses—but so it was in the era of the photocopier. Meanwhile, services have burgeoned, mostly open access, for a vast range of other communities of interest, for whom the Internet provides a natural home. Among these are fan networks connected to books, films, and TV programmes, knitting circles, working mums, and those brought together by adversity, such as sufferers from epilepsy or mental illness.

So far, so uncontroversial. But when it comes to communities of place, the traditional domain of the local newspaper, there is a continuing battle between new and established players as fierce as anything in the world of Big Media. The online newcomers in community news are often referred to as 'hyperlocal' news providers because of their ability to reach into the smallest geographical communities. Estimates of the scale of hyperlocal activity are sketchy in most countries, but an assessment provided by the UK communications regulator Ofcom in 2012 put the number of active sites in the UK at 432; a 46 per cent increase over the figure two years earlier. At the same time, the body representing UK local newspapers, the Newspaper Society, estimated that there were around 1,600 websites associated with local and regional newspapers. Ofcom research also suggested strongly growing levels of reliance on online information within communities. These sites may include blogs and news aggregation on web platforms such as Wordpress or

Ning. Others rely on Facebook pages as news and information hubs.

Research carried out by Nesta and by a number of journalism schools in Europe and North America paints a picture of a hyperlocals sector based mostly upon voluntary labour and small revenues, chiefly obtained from donations and grants, with a sprinkle of advertising and subscription. In the United States, commercial markets are better developed, encouraging the birth in 2007 of Patch, a New York-based network of hyperlocals benefiting from an aggregated offer to advertisers. Patch was sold for $7 million in 2009 to AOL, new owner of the Huffington Post and a willing investor in Patch's expansion, which by 2014 had taken Patch beyond the 1,000 site mark. This success provoked a feisty response from other hyperlocals styling themselves 'authentically local', drawing a distinction between their own independence and the corporate ownership of AOL. Although the term 'citizen journalist' is widely used among hyperlocals, it meets with objection from those who prefer to see themselves as activists or community builders, rather than journalists. A Nesta study into UK hyperlocals concluded that there was insufficient potential advertising revenue to support the type of aggregated advertising business model being pursued by Patch. Some AOL shareholders were sceptics from the beginning about the viability of Patch's business model, and in 2014 the business was put into a partnership with Hale Global, a business turnaround specialist, with severe cuts to its network and payroll.

For all of these disputes, however, the hyperlocals have brought tremendous new energy, ideas, and diversity to local news media at a time when conventional local newspapers were on the retreat. The Sheffield Forum, based in the UK's former steel industry capital, reached its tenth birthday with an impressive 150,000 regular users and 500,000 unique visitors monthly, despite or perhaps because of its rather dated web forum style. Successful hyperlocals in Karlruhe, Germany, and Warsaw used a 'city Wiki' platform to encourage collaboration, information sharing, and debate. A few hyperlocals have emerged from a base in television, and most hyperlocals are happy to work with text, images, audio, and video, using platforms like Audioboo, YouTube, and Flickr. A successful London site, the Brixton Blog, also launched the *Brixton Bugle* newspaper, one of several hyperlocals to reverse engineer into what some now call 'the Printernet'.

Willing to pay

A regular snapshot of the world of digital news across a number of countries is provided by the annual *Digital News Report* published by the Reuters Institute for the Study of Journalism at Oxford University. This study is able to compare patterns in different countries, finding that 'born-digital' brands for news are strongest in Japan and Brazil and weakest in the UK, Spain, and Germany. Broadcasters' online brands are exceptionally strong in the UK (a reflection of the funding strength of the BBC). This research also draws attention to the unsurprising but important fact that online sources of news are much more important for the under-44s than older people. The research shows the growing importance of mobile devices in news consumption and the ferment of change in the ways that audiences connect with news (see Figure 15).

WikiLeaks

If Matt Drudge bookends online journalism at the start of the 21st century, the figure who is perhaps best qualified to occupy that position 15 years later is Julian Assange, the Australian co-founder and frontman of WikiLeaks, established in 2006 as a countercultural online platform for anonymous whistleblowers (see Figure 16).

WikiLeaks's early revelations included material on Scientology, the illegal dumping of toxic waste, and the reckless dealings of Icelandic banks, but it was in April 2010 that WikiLeaks hit the

	UK	US	GER	FR	DEN	FIN	IT	BRA	SP	JPN
COMPUTER	57%	69%	60%	61%	54%	74%	69%	62%	63%	79%
MOBILE	24%	17%	24%	22%	24%	15%	19%	18%	22%	15%
TABLET	16%	10%	9%	8%	18%	9%	8%	8%	9%	3%

a) Main source digital news

	US	UK	GER	FR	DEN	FIN	SPA	ITA	BRA	JAP
BRAND	33%	45%	27%	22%	46%	57%	46%	39%	46%	20%
SEARCH	40%	29%	42%	40%	15%	26%	35%	59%	59%	41%
SOCIAL	28%	17%	15%	14%	16%	24%	38%	34%	46%	12%
EMAIL	27%	9%	12%	24%	16%	11%	12%	12%	22%	18%

b) Top gateways to news

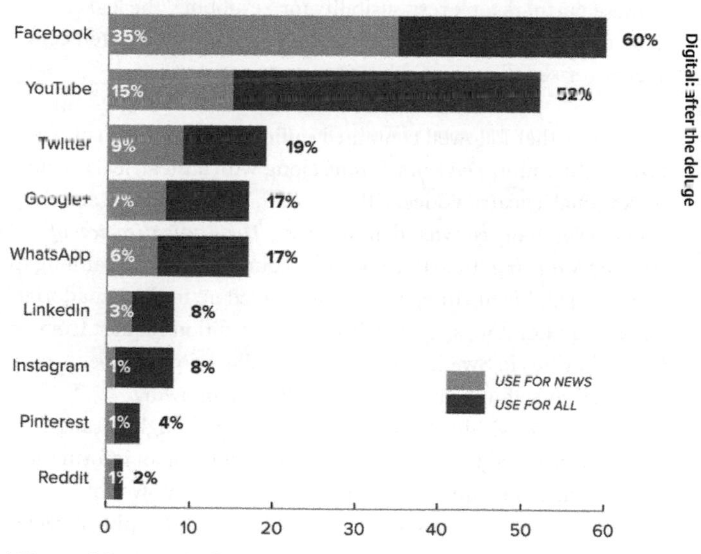

c) Top social networks for news

15. By the second decade of the century, news was increasingly consumed on mobile devices, as traditional news suppliers worked to re-assert their brands online

world's headlines, following publication of a video entitled *Collateral Murder*, an edited version of material shot from an American Apache helicopter during a controversial 2007 airstrike on Baghdad which resulted in the deaths of Iraqi citizens and two employees of the Reuters news agency. Soon afterwards, WikiLeaks published half a million documents concerning the wars in Afghanistan, followed by a haul of 250,000 diplomatic cables leaked from inside the American intelligence and diplomatic network.

In this enormous enterprise, WikiLeaks did not act alone. In order, it said, to amplify interest in this classified material, it formed partnerships with 50 media organizations around the world, among them the *New York Times* and the *Guardian*. Many of these partners took responsibility for 'scrubbing' the leaked data, to avoid the risk of putting the lives of individual intelligence agents at risk following publication.

The events that followed contained sufficient drama to inspire a 2013 feature film, *The Fifth Estate*, along with a theatrical account by National Theatre Wales of the life of the young American soldier eventually convicted of the leaks, *The Radicalisation of Bradley Manning*. In 2013, a military court sentenced Manning to 35 years' jail. Meanwhile, Assange was holed up in the Ecuadorian embassy in London, a fugitive from an extradition request from the authorities in Sweden concerning an allegation of rape. WikiLeaks itself was, by now, dysfunctional, following recriminations within the project's leadership, though Assange himself continued to emerge in public to condemn an information system which, he said, had put an unprecedented power of information in the hands of the authorities whilst keeping citizens in the dark.

Whatever your views about Assange's style and your judgements about his personal behaviour, WikiLeaks frames in a stark manner the toughest questions and challenges arising for journalism in

16. Julian Assange, founder of WikiLeaks, whose industrial-scale leaking of state secrets challenged governments and presented awkward questions for professional journalism

the digital era, where the people who call themselves journalists find themselves collaborating with the people formerly known as 'sources', as well as the people formerly known as the audience, to pursue journalism's long-standing ambition to hold power to account. WikiLeaks lays bare tensions previously negotiated only in private, as journalists and publishers agreed to secrecy for their sources and governments operated 'gentlemen's agreements' with the press over the protection of sensitive intelligence material. Even if you take the view that WikiLeaks is guilty of irresponsible treachery, meriting the strongest possible response from a punitive state, these issues are now here to stay and irreversibly recast. Big Data mean the continuous risk of Big Leaks, as proved to be the case when Edward Snowden, a former contract employee of the American National Security Agency, released an even larger store of information than WikiLeaks, in 2013, demonstrating that the American intelligence services listened into the mobile phone conversations of their closest allies and trawled the databanks of Internet service providers, social media networks, and other web platforms as a matter of course. Daniel Ellsberg, who was responsible in 1969 for a high-profile leakage of documents questioning the honesty of the official account of the conduct of the Vietnam War (the 'Pentagon Papers'), and who was, eventually, exonerated by the American courts, has made the case for a potential 'free expression' defence of WikiLeaks.

'The networked public sphere'

The arguments made on both sides of this debate are of the greatest importance. According to the Harvard-based legal scholar Yochai Benkler, what we are witnessing with WikiLeaks is the emergence of an aspect of the 'networked public sphere ... whose operations to some extent complement and to some extent compete with each other'. Benkler identifies these tensions at work in the relationship between the *New York Times*, with its well-established place in American society, and the anarchistic political culture of WikiLeaks. Bill Keller, executive editor of *The Times*, introduced a long essay for his newspaper's magazine by describing WikiLeaks as 'a secretive cadre of antisecrecy vigilantes', a remark Benkler objected to on the grounds that it played into the aggressive characterization of the American government's own reaction to WikiLeaks, which included pressing banks, credit card companies, and Internet companies to deny service to WikiLeaks, not to mention the legal pursuit of both Assange and Manning.

Benkler's conclusion is that WikiLeaks 'marks the emergence of a new model of watchdog function, one that is neither purely networked nor purely traditional, but is rather a mutualistic interaction between the two... Just as software companies had to learn to collaborate with open-source software developers, so too will this industry have to develop its interactions. Just as Wikipedia had to make the transition from laughing stock to indispensable part of life, so too with the 'networked fourth estate'.

WikiLeaks has also made an impact beyond the United States. For example, Assange has drawn attention to its role in Tunisia in partnership with an activist online group, Nawaat.org, where the content of cables damaging to the Ben Ali regime provided context for the first events of the 'Arab Spring'.

What, journalists ask each other, will history make of Julian Assange and Edward Snowden, one hiding in a London embassy, the other in Moscow? Will they, eventually, be punished and discredited, or will they be seen as leaders in the Internet-era phase of redefining rights to free expression and personal data privacy? Whichever view you take, it cannot be denied that these two issues are now so closely connected that the future of journalism, even the future of what we call democracy, is bound unbreakably to the future of the digital communications system we have built on the Internet. It is impossible to think about journalism's mission to hold power to account and its necessary core practice of verification without thinking about the mechanics of the Internet and the politics that shape the way it evolves.

A new politics of the machine

The problem and the beauty of the Internet are that there is no agreement about the international rules which should govern either its daily management or its strategic development. No fewer than 42 bodies compete for influence in this space, providing a running source of conflict between those states which are becoming increasingly skilled at managing their own 'national' Internet in their own way, as is most obvious in the case of China, though China is by no means alone.

For the United States and Europe, these conflicts provide new challenges to our understanding of free expression and its limits, though it cannot be assumed that even the United States and Europe will be in agreement on such matters. In 2014, European courts were making protective decisions about issues concerning personal privacy and intellectual property which would not have withstood scrutiny by American courts and, in the wake of the Snowden leaks, Europe moved to legislate for much tougher standards to protect private data than exist on the opposite side of the Atlantic. In debates I attended in 2013 and 2014 about the politics of the Internet, America was increasingly and surprisingly characterized as an 'outlier', albeit a hugely powerful one, in its potent combination of a constitutional commitment to free expression and an appetite for technological innovation which has put American companies at the commanding heights of the world's digital economy. Another source of running tensions arises in telecommunications regulation, where the concept of 'net neutrality' exists, in theory, to prevent discrimination between differing types of Internet traffic and with the wider goal of preserving a so-called 'open' Internet. Today there is growing evidence that this neutral stance is being adjusted to favour commercial ambitions, for example to ensure greater bandwidth for data-heavy media-streaming services. This adjustment is justified by pointing to the Internet's potential for supporting innovation and economic growth, which in turn requires heavy further investment in digital infrastructure. Other pressures on Internet governance arise from concerns about cybersecurity and the infringement of intellectual property rights. This is not the place to discuss such complex and wide-ranging issues. I mention them only to make the point that journalism, as was the case in the era of Gutenberg, is not the primary concern of the main protagonists in these debates; but its future shape will surely depend to a very considerable extent upon their outcome.

Gutenberg galaxy to internet galaxy

In the first edition of this book, I cited the sociologist Manuel Castells, whose great trilogy of books in the 1990s provided an early map of the 'network society'. Castells argued that the unique culture of the Internet would preserve it from takeover by corporations or emasculation by governments, so long as the Net's governance is not dominated by American interests. The Internet, he wrote, is 'a particularly malleable technology, susceptible of being deeply modifed by its social practice, and leading to a whole range of potential social outcomes—to be discovered by experience, not proclaimed beforehand…it is the expression of ourselves'. Castells suggested that 'if convergence takes place one day, it will be when the investment required in setting up broadband capabilities beyond the instrumental uses of the corporate world is justified by a new media system willing and ready to satisfy the most important latent demand: the demand for interactive free expression and autonomous creation—nowadays largely stymied by the sclerotic vision of the traditional media industry'.

These comments were prescient, but that has not prevented them from being overtaken by events. The Internet today almost defies rational discussion in terms of concepts such as 'governance'. In one sense, the Internet is indeed 'dominated by American interests', whether those of the American secret state and its political superstructure or its boundlessly innovative technology companies. For Europe, the risk is that a perfectly reasonable demand for inclusion in 'decisions about Internet governance' is distorted by a defensive, protectionist instinct provoked by fear of falling behind in the digital economy.

When, in March 2014, Sir Tim Berners-Lee, the man with the strongest claim to have invented the worldwide web, called for a 'Magna Carta'—a defining legal agreement—to secure the 'open Internet' as a global network available to everyone, including the majority of humankind yet to acquire meaningful access to it, the response has been an awkward silence which greets a man of vision, saying something with which no one wishes to disagree, but which lies beyond the reach of today's political realities. Here is not the place to try to see beyond this deadlock in the politics of the machine, but to note its vital importance to the question: What is journalism's future?

The age of the virus

I ended the first edition of this book with a Chinese proverb that 'the fish rots from the head', pointing to the dangers of failed leadership. I did so in order to make the point that this idea is out of time: we do not live in the age of secure, authoritarian leaderships but in the age of the virus, which strikes unpredictably from multiple directions and which cannot be resisted at a single point. This does not mean that we live in a compulsively democratic paradise, where tyranny is impossible, but it does mean that things happen in a viral manner, gathering pace quickly and subsiding only when a pattern of events has exhausted itself.

It is true to say that our news media ecology today, framed by the Internet and related digital communications technologies, is also viral. Barriers to entry are almost non-existent; anything goes and comes; and there is no single organization or individual to whom we can complain when the result displeases us. I argued in the first edition of this book that in a viral world, reliable, accurate, truthful, networked journalism is the only imaginable antidote and that this ecology of journalism would thrive only if we made sure that our commercial media markets are open and transparent, safeguarding competition and plurality, and sending clear signals when market failures occur, so that remedies can be considered through investment in public service journalism. Those points, I think, hold good.

What also has to be understood, however, is that politics itself, and statecraft, are changed by this new information ecology, not in a way that guarantees 'Facebook revolutions' against authoritarian leaders, but because democracy itself acquires a different shape, where 'parliamentary' and 'representative' democracy are insufficient. In an age of superabundant viral media, democracy becomes, in John Keane's term, 'monitory'—subject to inputs, advice, pressures, acts of leadership, devolved decision taking, and expressions of community of a very diverse kind. The digital communications revolution remakes politics, just as it remakes the news media.

For journalism, this has been very confusing. In the last 15 years, great news organizations have been broken up and good professional journalists have lost jobs which they did well. But what is emerging, as the news industry changes in response to digital technologies, and a host of new players innovate their way into contention, should not be greeted with anything other than guarded optimism. This new networked, or collaborative, or open, journalism is a mix of professional and amateur; some who practise it will not even call it journalism—they will think of themselves as activists, as specialists for whom 'journalism' is a by-product, or perhaps they will be regarded as a new breed of creative citizens. Professional journalists, called upon to collaborate with these newcomers, will need to be determined but also flexible about the goals of journalism. They will find that some of the old ideas and practices remain persuasive. In a working lifetime in and around journalism I have not found a better way of stating journalism's core mission than to call it: holding power to account. Journalists' most serious problems in the last 20 years have arisen from a reluctance to apply this insight to their own work. Journalism, in all its new and evolving forms, can only succeed in the mission of holding power to account if it is trusted and it will only be trusted if it embraces a discipline of checkable verification. As I said in the first edition, 'journalism must reabsorb the values of democracy into its own self-conduct'. To those who say that we are witnessing the death of journalism, I say that we surely are not. To those who wish to participate in journalism's reinvention, I say: the door is open.

Further reading

There has never been more writing and scholarship about journalism than there is today. With the boundaries of what defines 'journalism' and 'news' blown open by new technologies, writers from an increasingly diverse array of disciplines and perspectives have a place in this debate. You are as likely to find insights about the changing shape of news in the pages of *Wired* magazine or in the blogosphere as in books by journalism professors or professional journalists. This list invites catholic grazing.

Ken Auletta has written the outstanding 'Annals of Communication' column for *New Yorker* magazine since 1992.

Steven Barnett, *The Rise and Fall of Television Journalism* (London: Bloomsbury, 2011).

Benedetta Brevini et al. (eds), *Beyond WikiLeaks: Implications for the Future of Communications, Journalism and Society* (London: Palgrave Macmillan, 2013).

Michael Bromley and Tom O'Malley (eds), *A Journalism Reader* (London: Routledge, 1997) has key texts, including W. T. Stead's vision of 'government by journalism'.

Tim Burt, *Dark Art: The Changing Face of Public Relations* (London: Elliott and Thompson, 2012).

Manuel Castells, *The Internet Galaxy* (Oxford: Oxford University Press, 2001).

Simon Cottle, *Mediatized Conflicts* (Maidenhead: Open University Press, 2006): one of several good books on the news media, war, and other conflicts.

James Curran and Jean Seaton, *Power Without Responsibility: The Press and Broadcasting in Britain* (London: Routledge, 1997).

Nick Davies, *Flat Earth News* (London: Chatto and Windus, 2008).

Leonard Downie and Robert Kaiser, *The News about the News: American Journalism in Peril* (New York: Alfred A. Knopf, 2002): gloom from *The Washington Post*.

James Fallows, *Breaking the News: How the Media Undermine American Democracy* (London: Random House/Vintage, 1996).

Dan Gillmor, *We the Media: Grassroots Journalism by the People, for the People* (Sebastopol, CA: O'Reilly Media, 2006).

Roy Greenslade's blog for *Guardian* online (<http://www.theguardian.com/media/greenslade>). Other bloggers of note include Emily Bell of the Tow Centre for Digital Journalism and Jeff Jarvis (<http://www.buzzmachine.com>).

David Halberstam, *The Powers that Be* (New York: Alfred A. Knopf, 1979).

John Hartley, *Popular Reality: Journalism, Modernity, Popular Culture* (London: Arnold, 1996), along with his more recent work on digital cultures.

Graham Johnson, *Hack* (London: Simon and Schuster, 2012).

John Keane, *The Life and Death of Democracy* (London: Simon and Schuster, 2009).

Philip Knightley, *The First Casualty: The War Correspondent as Hero and Myth-Maker* (London: Prion, 2001) is a classic on this subject.

Bill Kovach and Tom Rosenstiel, *The Elements of Journalism: What Newspapers Should Know and the Public Should Expect* (New York: London Crown Publishing, 2001).

Larry Langman, *The Media in the Movies: A Catalogue of American Journalism Films 1900–1996* (Jefferson, NC: McFarland, 1998).

Plus Brian McNair, *Journalists in Film* (Edinburgh: Edinburgh University Press, 2010).

Walter Lippmann, *Public Opinion* (New York: Harcourt, Brace, 1922).

Walter Lippmann (ed.), *Washington Post Desk Book on Style* (New York: McGraw-Hill, 1989).

John Lloyd, *What the Media Are Doing to Our Politics* (London: Constable and Robinson, 2004) takes the politicians' side against worsening news media behaviour.

Robert McChesney and Victor Pickard (eds), 'Will the Last Reporter Please Turn Out the Lights: The Collapse of Journalism and What

Can Be Done to Fix It'. Note Yochai Benkler's contribution on 'the networked public sphere' (New York: New Press, 2011).
John Milton, *Areopagitica* (London, 1644).
George Orwell, *Essays* (London: Penguin, 2000): exemplary journalism.
Pew Center for People and the Press <http://www.people-press.org>: the leading American database and discussion zone on issues of news media standards.
Neil Postman, *Amusing Ourselves to Death* (New York: Viking Penguin, 1985).
Reuters Institute for the Study of Journalism: growing resource of accessible journalism research with a pan-European flavour (<http://www.reutersinstitute.politics.ox.ac.uk>). Linked to the European Journalism Observatory (<http://www.ejo.ch>).
Michael Schudson, *The Sociology of News* (New York: W.W. Norton. 2003).
Clay Shirky, *Here Comes Everybody* (New York: Penguin, 2008).
General Sir Rupert Smith, *The Utility of Force* (Cambridge: Polity, 2005).
John Stuart Mill, 'On Liberty', in *Utilitarianism*, ed. Geraint Williams (London: Everyman, 1972).
Evelyn Waugh, *Scoop* (London: Chapman and Hall, 1938).
David Weaver and Lars Willnat, *The Global Journalist in the 21st Century* (New York: Routledge, 2012).
Tom Wolfe, *The Purple Decades* (London: Jonathan Cape, 1983).
Mohamed Zayani and S. Sahraoui, *The Culture of Al Jazeera: Inside an Arab Media Giant* (Jefferson, NC: McFarland 2007).

Index

A

ABC television network 32
academic perspective on journalism 6–7, 26
Ace in the Hole (1951) 91
acquisitions 63–4, 72
activism 127
Adams, Eddie 36–7
advertising
- digital media 108, 110–11
- in early newspapers 15
- Internet 119, 122
- revenues from 2, 19, 65

Afghanistan 43
Agora (Polish publishing company) 76
Al Arabiya (television channel) 46
Al Jazeera 4, 30, 45–7, 48
al-Qaeda 44–5, 46
Algeria, deaths of journalists in 9
All the President's Men (1976) 92
Allbritton, Christopher 44
Amazon 2–3, 63
American Constitution 13, 20, 31
American Society of Newspaper Editors 98
Apple 2, 110
Arab Spring 30, 46, 135
Assange, Julian 130–3, 135
attention, holding the audience 40
attitudes towards journalists 1
Auden, W. H. 7
audience, monitoring 124

B

B92 (Belgrade radio station) 38–9
BAA 89
Babitsky, Andrei 25
Balkan wars 38–40
Baltimore Sun 82
Baxter, Leone 84–5
BBC (British Broadcasting Corporation) 3, 6, 31
- dominance 20
- employment of journalists 74
- ethical standards 95–6
- News website 39
- online services 113
- ownership 18
- 'sexing up' accusations 45

Bell, Martin 40
Benkler, Yochai 134–5
Bennett, Taylor 90
Berglez, Peter 104
Berlin Wall, fall of 1, 29
Berliner format 121
Berlusconi, Silvio (Italian prime minister) 32
Bernays, Edward 82, 83
Berners-Lee, Tim 138

Bertelsmann media group 67
Bezos, Jeff 2–3, 63, 72
Bild-Zeitung 52, 67, 113
Bin Laden, Osama 43
Black, Lord Conrad 64
Blair, Jayson 55
Blane, Torchy 91
blogging 44–5, 123–5
Bloomberg, Michael 64
Bolam, Silvester 52
Bosnian war 40
Bottomley, Horatio 88
Bourdieu, Pierre 32
Brazil, death of journalist in 8
British Journalism Review 100
broadband *see* Internet
Broadcast News (1987) 93
broadsheets 51, 121 *see also under individual titles*
Brokaw, Tom 41
Brown, Gordon 90
Burt, Tim 90
Bush, President George W. 41
Buzzfeed 61, 125–6

C

campaign management 85–7, 89–90
capitalism 22
Cardiff University 6–7
Carlton Television 55
Carrington, Colonel Edward 13
Castells, Manuel 137
CBS 19, 32
celebrities, journalists as 57–8, 117
celebrity culture 50–1, 55–9, 60–1
Censer, Jack Richard 14
censorship 22–3
  by journalists on themselves 97
  in war reporting 37, 38–9
Chandra, Subhash 65
China 3, 23, 27–9
  history of journalism 10
Chomsky, Noam 31
'churnalism' 81
Citizen Kane (1941) 67, 91
civic journalism 4
Clark, Gen. Wesley 39
Clinton, President Bill 22–3
  sex scandal 115–18
CNN (Cable News Network) 37, 64
Cockburn, Claud 79
coffee houses, early journalists working in 12
Columbia, deaths of journalists in 9
commercial broadcasting 19–20, 31–2
Committee of Concerned Journalists 72, 97
Committee to Protect Journalists (CPJ) 9
communications technologies 22–3, 37, 47–9
Communist Party
  China 27
  Russia 24
communities of interest 128
communities of place 128–30
competition law 73–4
consent, engineering 82–4
Constitution *see* American Constitution
Cooke, Janet 55
corporate ownership of media 18, 32–3, 62–77
corruption 100
Cottle, Simon 47
Coulson, Andy 107
Creel, George 82
crowdsourced funding 72
Cudlipp, Hugh 52
Cutlip, Scott 80
Czech Republic 32

D

Dacre, Paul 61, 120
Daily Herald 52

Daily Mail 61, 111–12, 120
Daily Mirror 52, 87, 111
Daily Telegraph 39
data journalism 123
Davies, Nick 80–1
deaths of journalists 8–9, 14, 26
Defoe, Daniel 12
demand media 81
democracy 17, 31–2, 139
demographics of journalists 101–3
Desmond, Richard 64
Dewey, John 17
Diana, Princess of Wales 56–7
Digital News Report 130
digital technologies 2, 4, 60–1, 108–11, 113–15, 119–40
  in war 47–9
dot-com boom 108–9
dot-com bust 109
Downie, Leonard 69
Drudge, Matt 6, 115–19

E

eBay 3
economic downturn 111–13
The Economist 123
editors
  controlled by media bosses 69–71
  long-standing 121
  responsibility 75–7
Editors' Code of Practice 95
Egypt 30
election campaigns 23–4
Ellsberg, Daniel 134
embedded journalists 44
English Civil War (1642–8) 12
Enquirer see *National Enquirer*
Enron 87–8
entertainment 50–1, 55–7, 60
  vs. information 31–2, 47, 51–2, 54, 59
Epstein, Gady 27–8
ethics 93–101, 103–7, 118
  financial 87–8
  see also morality
Europe
  media ownership 64–5
  press barons 67
  press regulation 33–4
  see also under individual countries
European Union (EU) 29
Evans, Harold 70
Evening Standard 123

F

Facebook 109–10
Falklands War 36–7, 53
Fallows, James 31
Federal Communications Commission (FCC) 19, 33
fictional news 53–5, 67, 83–4
fifth estate 114–15
The Fifth Estate (2013) 93, 133
films inspired by news stories 91–3
filter bubble 127
financial ethics 87–8
financial incentives 23
financial pressures 97
Financial Times 6, 74–5, 87–8, 120–1
Five Star Final (1931) 91–2
flak-catchers 79–80
Fleet Street, London 12–13
Fowler, Mark 19
France 13–14, 32, 113
free media 29
Freedom House 9–10, 11, 26
freedom of speech 14, 32
  on the Internet 136
freedom of the press 9–10, 11–15, 31–2, 106–7
  in Russia 25–6
French Revolution 13–14
The Front Page (1931) 91
Fukuyama, Francis 1
funding initiatives 72–3

G

Gannett 69
Gazeta Wyborcza 76
general election (May 1997) 85
General Strike (1926) 18
Germany 52, 67, 112–13
Giddens, Anthony 41
global journalism 104
globalization 1, 4
Glynn, Kevin 59
'golden era' of the press 15
Golden Shield system in China 27
Goodman, Clive 104
Google 2, 4, 65, 73–4, 109
Gould, Philip 86, 89
government
  control over television coverage 24–6
  media control 18, 20
  regulation *see* regulation
Great Chinese Firewall 27
Guardian 39–40, 71, 104, 121–2, 123, 132
Gulf War (1990–1) 37–8, 40
Gutenberg, Johannes 10–12

H

Hacked Off campaign 57
Halberstam, David 126
Harbrecht, Doug 117–18
Hart, Gary 54
Havel, Václav 32
headlines 53
Hearst, William Randolph 16, 51, 67, 91
Hetherington, Henry 15
Hill and Knowlton (PR company) 83–4
Hill, David 89
Hill, John 84, 86
Hillsborough disaster 53
history of journalism 10–21
Hollywood films 92–3
Huffington Post 125
Hussein, Saddam 43, 48
Hutton Report (January 2004) 45
hyperlocal news 128–30

I

impartiality 46
Independent 40, 75, 76–7, 123
India 3, 65
  deaths of journalists in 9
information
  vs. entertainment 31–2, 47, 51–2, 54, 59
  leaking 45, 49
  payments for 97
  regimes 22
  sources 79–85
  unlimited access on the Internet 114
infotainment 1, 31–2, 47, 50–1, 55–7, 60
inheritances 64
Insider, The (1998) 93
Internet
  access in China 27–9
  access in Russia 26
  blogging 44–5, 123–5
  diversity in journalism 76
  effect on journalism 109–11, 114–15, 119–24
  hyperlocal 128–30
  investment in news 2–4
  news formats 125–7
  opportunities for journalists 108
  regulation 136–8
  tabloid journalism 60–1
  viral media 126–7, 138–40
  war reporting 39, 48
investigative comedy 54
Iraq
  conflict 43–5
  deaths of journalists in 9

Italy 32
ITN (Independent Television News) 40

J

Japan 20–1
Jefferson, Thomas 13, 106
Johnson, Graham 94
Johnson, Hildy 100
Johnson, Senator Hiram 35, 45
journalists
affected by the Internet 139–40
as celebrities 57–8, 117
Chinese 28
deaths 8–9, 14, 26
decline in employment 111
Defoe's description of early 12
demographics 101–3
employers 74–7
ethical standards 97
loyalties 78
portrayed in films 93
W. T. Stead on 16
war reporting 35–44
working on the Internet 108

K

Kaiser, Robert 69
Kaldor, Mary 41
Kamp, David 59–60
Katz, Jon 99
Keane, John 139
Keller, Bill 134–5
Kennedy, Jackie 56
Khanfar, Wadah 47
Knightley, Philip 35
Koppel, Ted 38
Kovach, Bill 98–9, 100
Kurtz, Howard 87
Kuwait 83–4

L

Lady Gaga 60–1
Lambert, Richard 87–8
language use in war reporting 41, 42–3
Lebedev, Alexander 64
Lee, Ivy Ledbetter 82–3, 86
Leveson inquiry 33, 53, 57, 71, 86, 104–7
Lewinsky, Monica 115–18
Lewis, Arnold 93
libel 40
Liebling, A. J. 62
Lippmann, Walter 17, 83
Littlejohn, Richard 53
Liu Xiaobo 27
live blogging 123 *see also* blogging
Lloyd's List 111
LM (formerly *Living Marxism*) 40
local interest online media 128–30
local journalism 4
'Lord Copper' 67
Lukyanova, Irina 23–4
Lumby, Catharine 59
Lungren, Dan 59

M

McChesney, Robert 30
McCullin, Don 36
Mackenzie, Kelvin 52–3, 75, 94
McNair, Brian 93
magazines, online subscriptions 122–3
Mail Online 120 *see also Daily Mail*
Manning, Chelsea (Bradley) 45, 132
Marat, Jean Paul 14
Marinho, Robert 65
market-based journalism 17–18
Massad, Joseph 30
Maxwell, Robert 64

media control 18, 20, 22–3, 24–6
media ownership 18, 32–3, 62–77
'mediatized war' 47–9
mergers 72
Metro 123
Mexico, deaths of journalists in 9
Meyer, Eugene 94
Michnik, Adam 76
Middle East
  Al Jazeera 4, 30, 45–7, 48
  political change 30
Miliband, David 89
Mill, James 14
Mill, John Stuart 14
Milton, John 12
Minow, Newton 19
Mirror see *Daily Mirror*; *New York Mirror*
mobile communication 47–9
monopoly publishing 18, 20
Moore, Michael 54
morality
  differences between workplaces 101
  issues of consent 82–4
  public perception 97
  suspicion of journalists 1
  see also ethics
Morgan, Piers 86, 87
Mulgan, Geoff 86
Murdoch, Rupert 20, 22, 52–3, 64, 69–71, 86, 104–5
Murrow, Ed 19

N

National Enquirer 53–4, 56, 57
NATO 38, 39
NBC 32–3, 45
Neto, Rodrigo 8
'New Journalism' 15–16, 99
New Statesman 6, 75, 85, 123
New York Enquirer 53
  see also National Enquirer
New York Mirror 51
New York Times 31, 45, 46, 55, 72, 122, 132, 134–5
New Yorker 123
Newhouse, Samuel Irving (Si) 64
news
  fictional 53–5, 67, 83–4
  hyperlocal 128–30
  information vs. entertainment 31–2, 47, 51–2, 54, 59
  inspiration for films 91–3
  online 130
  payments for 97
  spread on the Internet 109–10
news agencies 15
News of the World 53, 70–1, 101, 104–5
newspapers
  Chinese 28–9
  decline 111–13
  early 15
  effect of digital technologies 2
  ethical standards 94–5, 96
  format 121
  Jefferson's support of 13
  local 128, 130
  online subscriptions 119–22
  power over politicians 17
  Russian 24
  tabloid 51–7
  vs. television news coverage 18
  titles 16
  war reporting 39–40
  websites 61
Newsweek magazine 111, 115
Northcliffe doctrine 78–9
NTV (Russian television station) 24–5
Nye, Joseph 89

O

Obama, President Barack 41
Ofcom (Office of Communications) 33, 107, 128
Omidyar, Pierre 3

O'Neill, Dr Onora 100
The Onion 51
open journalism 121
Ostankino broadcasting complex, Russia 24–5
ownership, media 18, 32–3, 62–77

P

Paine, Thomas 13
Pakistan, deaths of journalists in 8–9
Pall Mall Gazette 15–16
paparazzi 56–7 *see also* tabloid journalism; tabloid press
Parisier, Eli 127
Patch 129
Pearl, Daniel 8–9
Peretti, Jonah 125–6
Pew Centre for the People and the Press 60, 99, 111
Philippines, deaths of journalists in 9
phone hacking scandal 71, 104–7
political scandals 54
politicians
  and the Leveson inquiry 106–7
  control over television coverage 23
  relationship with journalists 86
politics
  affected by viral media 139
  campaign management 85–7, 89–90
  celebrities' views 61
  influence on media barons 64–5
Politkovskaya, Anna 26
Poor Man's Guardian 15
Pope, Generoso Jr. 53–4, 56
Postman, Neil 31, 51
Poynter Institute 94
Pravda 22
press barons 62–73
  see also Murdoch, Rupert
Press Club 117–18
Press Complaints Commission (PCC) 95–7, 104, 106
press freedom 9–10, 11–15, 31–2, 106–7
  Russia 25–6
  see also freedom of speech
Press Gazette 112
press regulation *see* regulation
printing technology, invention 10–12
Private Eye 122–3
Project for Excellence in Journalism 97
propaganda 31, 81–2
  war reporting 35–45
Prouvost, Jean 67
public journalism 4
public perception of morality 97
public relations companies 88–90
  as sources of information 80–5
Public Relations Society of America 84
public service corporations 74
  see also BBC
publishers 17
Pulitzer, Joseph 16
Pulitzer Prize 125
Putin, President Vladimir 4, 23, 25–6

R

radio, war reporting 38–9
Rag Trade (2005) 93
RAI (Italian broadcasting system) 32
Rapaczynski, Wanda 76
recession 2
Reformation 12
regulation 53, 57, 106–7
  of broadcasting 33–4
  competition law 73–4
  Internet 136–8
  of the press 71
Reith, John 18

religion, influence on early
journalism 12
reporters
live 123
on location 58
reputation 88–90
riots (UK, 2011) 123–4
Rockefeller, John D. Jr 82
role of journalism 7
Rolling Stone magazine 99
Rosen, Jay 109
Rosenstiel, Tom 71–2, 98–9, 100
Rusbridger, Alan 121–2
Russia 4, 21–2, 23–6
deaths of journalists in 9

S

Sakr, Naomi 30
Salam Pax 44
salary of journalists 102–3
Sambrook, Richard 58
Schudson, Michael 10, 17
sensationalism 15, 52–5, 106
September 11 attacks (2001) 41, 42–3, 45
Seymour-Ure, Colin 69
Sheffield Forum 129
Shehadi, Nadim 46
Shirky, Clay 114
Simpson, O. J., trial 59
SkaT (Russian television station) 23
Sloan, Bill 54
Smith, Gen. Sir Rupert 36
Smith, William Wolff 82
Snowden, Edward 49, 134, 135
social media 44–5, 49, 60–1, 109–10
as source of information 81
public relations 88
see also Internet
Somalia, deaths of journalists in 9
soundbites 40
special interest online media 128
spin doctors 85–7, 89–90
Springer, Axel 67–8
stamp duty 15
Stead, W. T. 15–16
suicides as result of news stories 93–4
Sullivan, Andrew 124–5
Sulzberger family 122
Sun 52–3, 111
Sunday Times 57
Syria, deaths of journalists in 9
Syrian war 36

T

tabloid journalism 51–7, 59–61
online 126
tabloid press 15–17, 68
ethics 93–4
Leveson inquiry 33, 53, 57, 71, 86, 104–7
Taliban 43
television 113
Arabic-language 4, 30, 45–7, 48
commercial 19–20, 31–2
corporate ownership 32–3
effect of Internet 120
entertainment on 51
news coverage 18–20
news presenters 57–8
politicians on 23
Russian 23, 24–6
tabloid journalism 59–60
war footage 36, 37–8
terrorism 41, 42
Thatcher, Margaret 20, 53
The Times 15, 39, 112
Time Magazine 126
Time Warner 108–9
titles of newspapers 16
Trnopolje camp, Bosnia 40

trust, public 88–90 *see also* spin doctors
truth
  accounts of 59
  deviating from 83–4
  ethical standards 94, 99, 100–1
  exposition 78–81
  lacking in tabloid press 53–5, 57
  spin 89
  in war reporting 35–40
Turner, Ted 64
Twitter 60–1, 110
Twopenny Dispatch 15

U

United States 30
  Al Jazeera in 47, 48
  changes in news industry 1–4
  Constitution 13, 20, 31
  corporate ownership of media 32–3
  decline of newspapers 113
  ethical standards 97–9
  flak-catchers 79
  hyperlocal news 129
  media ownership 64
  press regulation 33–4
  television news coverage 19, 20
  yellow press 16–17, 118
Upworthy 126–7

V

Vietnam War 36–7
viral media 126–7, 138–40

W

Wall Street Journal 72
Walters, Barbara 57
War Crimes trials 39
'War on Terror' 41, 43
war reporting 35–45, 47–8
war zones 8
warblogs 44–5
Washington Post 3, 58, 63, 69, 72, 92–3, 101
  Desk Book on Style 94–5
Watergate scandal 92–3
Waugh, Evelyn 67
Weaver, Professor David 103
whistleblowers 45, 130, 135
Whitaker, Clem 84–5
WikiLeaks 45, 130–36
Wikipedia 115
Winfrey, Oprah 59
Wolfe, Tom 79
World Association of Press Councils 96
Wright, Hamilton 84

Y

Yakhontov, Alexander 24
yellow press 16–17, 118
Yugoslavia, Balkan wars 38–40

Z

Zassoursky, Ivan 26
Zenith Media, list of top media companies 65–6

Expand your collection of

VERY SHORT INTRODUCTIONS

1. Classics
2. Music
3. Buddhism
4. Literary Theory
5. Hinduism
6. Psychology
7. Islam
8. Politics
9. Theology
10. Archaeology
11. Judaism
12. Sociology
13. The Koran
14. The Bible
15. Social and Cultural Anthropology
16. History
17. Roman Britain
18. The Anglo-Saxon Age
19. Medieval Britain
20. The Tudors
21. Stuart Britain
22. Eighteenth-Century Britain
23. Nineteenth-Century Britain
24. Twentieth-Century Britain
25. Heidegger
26. Ancient Philosophy
27. Socrates
28. Marx
29. Logic
30. Descartes
31. Machiavelli
32. Aristotle
33. Hume
34. Nietzsche
35. Darwin
36. The European Union
37. Gandhi
38. Augustine
39. Intelligence
40. Jung
41. Buddha
42. Paul
43. Continental Philosophy
44. Galileo
45. Freud
46. Wittgenstein
47. Indian Philosophy
48. Rousseau
49. Hegel
50. Kant
51. Cosmology
52. Drugs
53. Russian Literature
54. The French Revolution
55. Philosophy
56. Barthes
57. Animal Rights
58. Kierkegaard
59. Russell
60. Shakespeare
61. Clausewitz
62. Schopenhauer
63. The Russian Revolution
64. Hobbes
65. World Music
66. Mathematics
67. Philosophy of Science
68. Cryptography
69. Quantum Theory
70. Spinoza
71. Choice Theory
72. Architecture
73. Poststructuralism
74. Postmodernism
75. Democracy

76. Empire
77. Fascism
78. Terrorism
79. Plato
80. Ethics
81. Emotion
82. Northern Ireland
83. Art Theory
84. Locke
85. Modern Ireland
86. Globalization
87. The Cold War
88. The History of Astronomy
89. Schizophrenia
90. The Earth
91. Engels
92. British Politics
93. Linguistics
94. The Celts
95. Ideology
96. Prehistory
97. Political Philosophy
98. Postcolonialism
99. Atheism
100. Evolution
101. Molecules
102. Art History
103. Presocratic Philosophy
104. The Elements
105. Dada and Surrealism
106. Egyptian Myth
107. Christian Art
108. Capitalism
109. Particle Physics
110. Free Will
111. Myth
112. Ancient Egypt
113. Hieroglyphs
114. Medical Ethics
115. Kafka
116. Anarchism
117. Ancient Warfare
118. Global Warming
119. Christianity
120. Modern Art
121. Consciousness
122. Foucault
123. The Spanish Civil War
124. The Marquis de Sade
125. Habermas
126. Socialism
127. Dreaming
128. Dinosaurs
129. Renaissance Art
130. Buddhist Ethics
131. Tragedy
132. Sikhism
133. The History of Time
134. Nationalism
135. The World Trade Organization
136. Design
137. The Vikings
138. Fossils
139. Journalism
140. The Crusades
141. Feminism
142. Human Evolution
143. The Dead Sea Scrolls
144. The Brain
145. Global Catastrophes
146. Contemporary Art
147. Philosophy of Law
148. The Renaissance
149. Anglicanism
150. The Roman Empire
151. Photography
152. Psychiatry
153. Existentialism
154. The First World War
155. Fundamentalism
156. Economics
157. International Migration
158. Newton
159. Chaos
160. African History
161. Racism

162. Kabbalah
163. Human Rights
164. International Relations
165. The American Presidency
166. The Great Depression and The New Deal
167. Classical Mythology
168. The New Testament as Literature
169. American Political Parties and Elections
170. Bestsellers
171. Geopolitics
172. Antisemitism
173. Game Theory
174. HIV/AIDS
175. Documentary Film
176. Modern China
177. The Quakers
178. German Literature
179. Nuclear Weapons
180. Law
181. The Old Testament
182. Galaxies
183. Mormonism
184. Religion in America
185. Geography
186. The Meaning of Life
187. Sexuality
188. Nelson Mandela
189. Science and Religion
190. Relativity
191. The History of Medicine
192. Citizenship
193. The History of Life
194. Memory
195. Autism
196. Statistics
197. Scotland
198. Catholicism
199. The United Nations
200. Free Speech
201. The Apocryphal Gospels
202. Modern Japan
203. Lincoln
204. Superconductivity
205. Nothing
206. Biography
207. The Soviet Union
208. Writing and Script
209. Communism
210. Fashion
211. Forensic Science
212. Puritanism
213. The Reformation
214. Thomas Aquinas
215. Deserts
216. The Norman Conquest
217. Biblical Archaeology
218. The Reagan Revolution
219. The Book of Mormon
220. Islamic History
221. Privacy
222. Neoliberalism
223. Progressivism
224. Epidemiology
225. Information
226. The Laws of Thermodynamics
227. Innovation
228. Witchcraft
229. The New Testament
230. French Literature
231. Film Music
232. Druids
233. German Philosophy
234. Advertising
235. Forensic Psychology
236. Modernism
237. Leadership
238. Christian Ethics
239. Tocqueville
240. Landscapes and Geomorphology
241. Spanish Literature
242. Diplomacy

243. North American Indians
244. The U.S. Congress
245. Romanticism
246. Utopianism
247. The Blues
248. Keynes
249. English Literature
250. Agnosticism
251. Aristocracy
252. Martin Luther
253. Michael Faraday
254. Planets
255. Pentecostalism
256. Humanism
257. Folk Music
258. Late Antiquity
259. Genius
260. Numbers
261. Muhammad
262. Beauty
263. Critical Theory
264. Organizations
265. Early Music
266. The Scientific Revolution
267. Cancer
268. Nuclear Power
269. Paganism
270. Risk
271. Science Fiction
272. Herodotus
273. Conscience
274. American Immigration
275. Jesus
276. Viruses
277. Protestantism
278. Derrida
279. Madness
280. Developmental Biology
281. Dictionaries
282. Global Economic History
283. Multiculturalism
284. Environmental Economics
285. The Cell
286. Ancient Greece
287. Angels
288. Children's Literature
289. The Periodic Table
290. Modern France
291. Reality
292. The Computer
293. The Animal Kingdom
294. Colonial Latin American Literature
295. Sleep
296. The Aztecs
297. The Cultural Revolution
298. Modern Latin American Literature
299. Magic
300. Film
301. The Conquistadors
302. Chinese Literature
303. Stem Cells
304. Italian Literature
305. The History of Mathematics
306. The U.S. Supreme Court
307. Plague
308. Russian History
309. Engineering
310. Probability
311. Rivers
312. Plants
313. Anaesthesia
314. The Mongols
315. The Devil
316. Objectivity
317. Magnetism
318. Anxiety
319. Australia
320. Languages
321. Magna Carta
322. Stars
323. The Antarctic
324. Radioactivity
325. Trust
326. Metaphysics

327. The Roman Republic
328. Borders
329. The Gothic
330. Robotics
331. Civil Engineering
332. The Orchestra
333. Governance
334. American History
335. Networks
336. Spirituality
337. Work
338. Martyrdom
339. Colonial America
340. Rastafari
341. Comedy
342. The Avant-Garde
343. Thought
344. The Napoleonic Wars
345. Medical Law
346. Rhetoric
347. Education
348. Mao
349. The British Constitution
350. American Politics
351. The Silk Road
352. Bacteria
353. Symmetry
354. Marine Biology
355. The British Empire
356. The Trojan War
357. Malthus
358. Climate
359. The Palestinian-Israeli Conflict
360. Happiness
361. Diaspora
362. Contemporary Fiction
363. Modern War
364. The Beats
365. Sociolinguistics
366. Food
367. Fractals
368. Management
369. International Security
370. Astrobiology
371. Causation
372. Entrepreneurship
373. Tibetan Buddhism
374. The Ancient Near East
375. American Legal History
376. Ethnomusicology
377. African Religions
378. Humour
379. Family Law
380. The Ice Age
381. Revolutions
382. Classical Literature
383. Accounting
384. Teeth
385. Physical Chemistry
386. Microeconomics
387. Landscape Architecture
388. The Eye
389. The Etruscans
390. Nutrition
391. Coral Reefs
392. Complexity
393. Alexander the Great
394. Hormones
395. Confucianism
396. American Slavery
397. African American Religion
398. God
399. Genes
400. Knowledge
401. Structural Engineering
402. Theatre
403. Ancient Egyptian Art and Architecture
404. The Middle Ages
405. Materials
406. Minerals
407. Peace
408. Iran
409. World War II
410. Child Psychology
411. Sport